Dear Reader,

I am a homeschooling mother of five. My family and I love to travel and want to learn about the world by being in it. After many trips that felt wasted, I began to accept that we would have to visit everything twice to be satisfied. Once to see what was there, and a second time to take advantage of it.

"We would have studied this if we'd known it was here," seemed to become the motto of our family vacations. I decided it shouldn't be that way, there should be materials available for families like mine, and I began to work on the idea for the Vacation Education Book series.

More than a where to stay and what to eat travel guide, this is a book that helps parents decide what their family will bring home from the trip (and we're not just talking souvenirs.)

I hope that you will find this like a letter from a friend, and that it will help your family make the most of your time together wherever you are. Even more, I hope that you will write back and let me know what you think.

CORINNE

Come visit us at

VACATIONEDUCATIONBOOKS.COM

The time has come again... time to plan your family vacation. Where will you go? What will you see? What will you do? How will you spend your hard earned money?

So many questions to answer... and the answers matter more now than they ever have before. In an age where everyone is doing their own thing; the girls have dance, the boys have sports, Mom's got a meeting and Dad's working late. That's just Monday's list. Every night of the week there seems to be something. More and more families are segregated by age, gender and interest. The only family activity left is the annual family vacation. How you spend it is really important, but the answers to the most important questions are often neglected until the vacation is over.

- Did everyone in the family benefit from this trip?
- Have we gained something from the time spent together?
- Have we been educated? Edified? Encouraged?
- Will we remember this time together fondly?
- Have we strengthened our relationships with one another?

How would you have answered these questions after your last vacation? Are you satisfied with those answers? How will you answer them next time?

With this book and a little planning, your next vacation will be the best one yet!

Have you ever been sight seeing and thought, "Wow! What a great exhibit! The kids are really interested in this, I wish we knew more about it."?

It happens to everyone. Families everywhere watch helplessly as precious teachable moments pass them by.

- Are you tired of fighting with kids about homework assignments?
- Do you want to get away without feeling guilty for "skipping" school? Without worrying about lessons the kids have missed?
- Are you looking for a vacation that provides lasting benefits?
- Are you ready for something more substantial than a roller coaster ride?

YOU NEED

VACATION EDUCATION: MAGIC KINGDOM
Take a peek at US history through a cloud of pixie dust

Vacation Education is exactly what the name implies, a vacation from traditional education. Every destination we explore as a family provides a platform from which to build a learning experience. It's time to take advantage of these. It's time to let your vacation destination provide the education. This book will give you all the tools necessary to implement a successful unit study based on your trip to the Magic Kingdom.

VACATION EDUCATION
Destination
MAGIC KINGDOM
With links to MGM Studios
And other parks

By: Corinne Lyn Johnson

U.S. History sprinkled with pixie dust

Table of Contents

How To Use This Book

Walt Disney World's Magic Kingdom (sometimes referred to as MK from here on in) is one of the most popular vacation destinations in the world. There's Mickey Mouse and Donald Duck and Goofy too; all your favorite old characters, plus many new ones, like Nemo and Ariel. If you are buying this book as part of the VACATION EDUCATION series, you might figure EPCOT was the obvious educational choice, but Magic Kingdom? What could we possibly learn here? Educational is not the first word that pops into my mind when I think of this vacation destination. However, because of the abundant requests to add MK to our series as a partner book for EPCOT, and our honest belief that there is potential for learning everywhere you go, we decided to go for it. We began with the obvious historical elements and worked our way from there.

This park is designed in a hub and spoke system, Cinderella's castle is the hub, and the spokes are the paths leading to each of the lands. There are touring plans available (We recommend "The Unofficial Guide to Walt Disney World" as the best source for these) to guide you through the park in the most efficient way, so that you have the shortest possible wait times and are able to accomplish the most in one day. Vacation Education destination MK will take you through the history portrayed in the park in the most efficient way - chronologically.

Beginning in Fantasyland, we'll discover the myths, legends, and fairy tales that Walt Disney and others in his generation grew up listening to as bedtime stories and how they influenced his design for Disneyland.

Our next stop on this journey will be Liberty Square, a peek into the beginnings of our country and it's independence. The descendants of the brave men and women who began this nation will go on to brave the untamed west, and we'll learn about them when we venture into Frontierland. Those wild journeys would lead to the exploration of untamed jungles, and newly discovered lands and we'll tell those tales (some true, some greatly exaggerated) as we go on our own exploration through the exhibits in Adventureland.

Our journey will be nearly over as we visit Main Street, USA and discover subtle clues to the past in this turn of the century downtown. Next, we'll learn about the magic that Walt brought to the stories he told, how Mickey Mouse came to be and we'll take a peek into Mickey's Toon Town Fair to say hello to some of your favorite characters. From the early 1900's, we jump forward to Tomorrowland and discover the limitless possibilities that our future may hold.

Prepare for an adventure... studying history at the Magic Kingdom is like getting a glimpse into the past through a cloud of pixie dust.

We are about to begin.

Please remain seated with your arms and legs inside the ride car at all times...

Links to the Studios

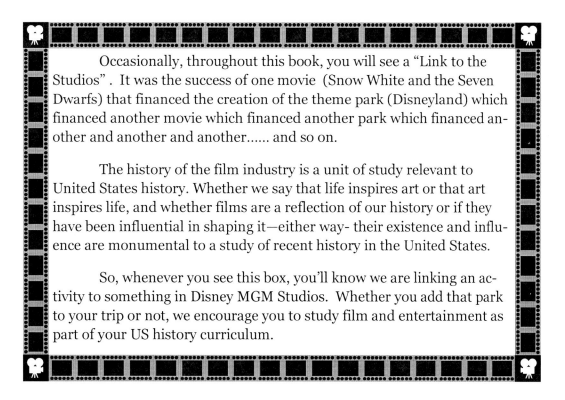

Occasionally, throughout this book, you will see a "Link to the Studios". It was the success of one movie (Snow White and the Seven Dwarfs) that financed the creation of the theme park (Disneyland) which financed another movie which financed another park which financed another and another and another...... and so on.

The history of the film industry is a unit of study relevant to United States history. Whether we say that life inspires art or that art inspires life, and whether films are a reflection of our history or if they have been influential in shaping it—either way- their existence and influence are monumental to a study of recent history in the United States.

So, whenever you see this box, you'll know we are linking an activity to something in Disney MGM Studios. Whether you add that park to your trip or not, we encourage you to study film and entertainment as part of your US history curriculum.

Activity Key

All of the activities in this book are divided into the following categories:

Find Out! Students are asked to research a topic.

Try It! These activities involve hands on or active learning tasks.

Taste it! New foods and recipes to try.

Did You Know? There are interesting facts and trivia here.

Check it out! These ask students to learn more about something.

Share it! (previously Show Off!) This is an opportunity to use what you've learned, and share your knowledge with others.

Line Time! Suggestions to make time fly when you're stuck in line.

Don't Forget! Use those vocabulary lists! Use these as search words on the internet, add them to your spelling list, and look them up in the card catalog to see what you can find. There is space available for you to write in your own words that you discover along the way.

The original purpose of these books was to provide the background information to fuel a series of unit studies all based on exhibits inside the park. MK becomes the central field trip to top off a year of exciting learning. Many of the educational activities can be done before you go or after you return.

Families planning a Disney vacation, who already have a planned curriculum (be it one of your own choosing or one chosen by your child's school) may not have ample time or desire to take advantage of everything that this book has to offer. Instead, you will be able to read the material and add to your children's interest and knowledge as you explore the park..

Homeschool families who are looking for a fun and interactive way to explore a subject will appreciate this book, even if they never go to Walt Disney World.

Don't Go Yet... 10 Things To Think About Before You Even Pack

1. **Disney parks require a lot of walking**.
   The combination of exercise and heat (which Florida has a lot of) creates rapid calorie burning and fluid loss. Start walking every day as a family as much in advance of your trip as possible. Every little bit helps. The more prepared your body is the less breaks you'll need, and the more sights you'll get to see. Also, plan to drink plenty of water, and be sure everyone has comfortable walking shoes.

   "Sandals and flip-flops lead to blisters and band-aids."

2. **Post a master list of what to pack, and what tasks need to happen before leaving home.**
   Who will check on the plants and pets? Who will check the mail? Does anyone know how to reach you in case of an emergency? Will you be leaving anyone behind? Taking someone else's child with you? Put medical information in writing. Cross each item off your list as it's completed.

   "Fanny packs are great for small snacks like nuts and raisins... [these help] keep everyone's energy up between meals."

3. **TRY IT!** **Prepare a Countdown Calendar for your trip.** You will need; paper cut into strips, tape, and a pen.

Step One: Write "And we're off!" or something similar on the first strip.
Step Two: Roll the strip so that the ends meet and the writing is on the inside. Tape the ends together.
Step Three: Write "One More Day" on the second strip, and a special activity to be done that day, like "Today, we pack the car. You can help!"
Step Four: Repeat step two, first looping the strip into the previously made ring, so that you begin to have a chain. When you have a whole row of rings, attach the first one to the wall in a conspicuous location. Each day, your child can take one down and read the message. Then, do the fun activity together. Here are some suggestions:

"This string of rings is a visual reminder to help your children answer for themselves the constant question "How many more days until we go to Disney World?""

10 more days, Let's go to www.disneyworld.com and pick our favorite attractions. What do you want to see first?
5 more days, Let's rent a Disney movie. Which one is your favorite?
4 days to go, where is the camera? Let's pack film and batteries too.
3 days to go, have you started packing yet? Let's pick out our favorite summer clothes. Don't forget the sun block.

"The countdown calendar really does keep little ones from going bonkers waiting for the big day."

4. Call Them. You can reach Disney at 1-407-WDISNEY and request their vacation planning package. You should do this at least a few weeks before your scheduled trip. They will provide you with free brochures, and a DVD to get your group excited. This is a helpful tool whether you book a package through Disney or not.

At 1-407-WDWTOURS you can ask to be included in a park tour while you are there. This is especially fun for returning guests who think they've seen and done it all, as it adds a whole new perspective to the park. Tours require reservations and a fee in addition to the park admission, so be sure to get all the details when you call.

If you are planning to have any special meals while you are visiting the parks, and want to make sure that you can get a table at your favorite restaurant, call 1-407-WDW-DINE to make priority seating reservations.

TIP: If you booked your vacation through Disney, you can go to their web site and plan your itinerary. Once you do this, request a free personalized map of each park. They will send it to you in the mail. You decide what's on your map. When it arrives, it even has your name on it.

"This map is a very cool souvenir... and it's free!"

5. Put together an emergency kit for your trip. Make sure that everyone in your group knows what to do in case of an emergency. Be prepared for luggage mishaps (they happen). Contact the airline and find out how early you will need to arrive at the airport, and what kinds of paperwork or identification they require. Ask about restrictions they have concerning carry ons. For security reasons, some items may not be allowed on the plane.

6. If you go during a busy season, you will need to understand how a Fast Pass works in order to see all the things you want to see. Here's a quickie lesson: You approach Space Mountain and the line is long, say 45 minutes. You look at the clock (there is one posted at the Fast Pass booth) and it says 10:00. Fast Pass return time (also posted here) says 11:00 -11:30. You insert your park entrance ticket (each person in your group must do this) and the machine spits out a Fast Pass ticket. You go sit in the shade, get a drink, take some pictures, look for items on your scavenger hunt list, see a couple of attractions that have shorter lines, and return to Space Mountain at 11:25. The line now has a 90 minute wait, but you enter through the Fast Pass holders gate with your Fast Pass ticket, and you are shown to the front of the line. You won't actually get to ride any sooner in the day, but you won't have to spend your wait time standing in line.

MK is designed for all ages, and has only five attractions with height requirements. Disney parks offer "Baby Swap" for these. It is similar to the Fast Pass. Example: Your group approaches the entrance and you tell the cast member that you want to Baby Swap. They will hand you a pass. Part of your group gets in line and goes on the ride, while someone stays with the baby. You meet at the exit, pass off the baby and the waiting party gets to go through the Fast Pass line.

7. **Plan to bring home lasting souvenirs.** We recommend books and pictures; everything else seems to end up in the annual yard sale.

8. Pack a stopwatch. Let the kids take turns timing things while they are standing in line. Might I suggest something other than how long you have to stand in line; How long can everyone go without talking? Compete to break each other's records. If you can see the ride going by, how much time passes between ride cars, is it always the same? How long does it take for the attraction to load and unload? For added interest, have everyone take a guess at how long they think something will take, then time it to see who came the closest.

9. Check out our Traveling Tips and Tidbits. Towards the back of the book, we've included some traveling games and other funs items. These are not park specific, just some extra fun things we wanted to share with you to help make all your travels more enjoyable.

10. ONE FINAL NOTE TO PARENTS

There is much to learn from the exhibits and attractions in Walt Disney World's Magic Kingdom, and we encourage you to take advantage of it all, but it must be tempered with the Truth. What you see here is Disneyfied, and fantasized, not intended to be a picture of reality. We have tried to temper the fantasy with Biblical truth throughout this book, but believe as parents, it is your responsibility to give your children a strong foundation in God's Word, and discernment so that nothing will cause them to stumble.

Please read the book of Deuteronomy and pray for God's design for your family and for the teaching of your children.

Deut 4:9 (NIV) Only be careful, and watch yourselves closely so that you do not forget the things your eyes have seen or let them slip from your heart as long as you live. Teach them to your children and to their children after them. 4:10 Remember the day you stood before the LORD your God at Horeb, when he said to me, "Assemble the people before me to hear my words so that they may learn to revere me as long as they live in the land and may teach them to their children."

Our responsibility is not just to provide proper training and instruction for our own children, but also to provide the training and instruction that will enable them to train and instruct our grandchildren. What a great privilege and calling for parents!

What If I Don't Know How To Do A Unit Study?

Wherever your child learns, be it a public or private institution, or in the comfort of his own home, he has probably experienced some form of a unit study (even if neither of you knew it). Perhaps his class studied Native Americans (history), and built teepees (math, construction, engineering), evaluated a tribes hunting patterns (math, science, conservation), and tried a recipe or two (math and science). Students may have been asked to research tribes that once lived near their current home, and create a presentation. This assignment would likely include elements of art, reading, writing, and public speaking in addition to history, and social sciences.

'Unit study' is just a way of expressing the steps one would normally take to obtain knowledge about a specific topic, and incorporating a variety of academic subjects into the study of that topic. These are gaining popularity among educators and parents because they so accurately simulate the way children naturally learn. A variety of subjects such as art, science, math, history and language are all covered when we venture to find out how trains really work. Imagine this: A family crowds around the computer oohing and aahing at the WDW (Walt Disney World) website as they check out Magic Kingdom's Big Thunder Mountain Railroad. Dad just read this book and begins to discuss the back story of this attraction (an abandoned gold mine), and someone asks, "What was the gold rush like?" The next thing they know, the whole family is on an adventure through cyberspace to figure it out, and they don't even realize they are doing "school".

Sound to simple? Here's a true story of unit study success.

> *Our fourth grader cried at the sight of her math book until we replaced it with a cookbook. After two weeks of menu planning, budgeting, doubling recipes and creating nutritional meals, fractions no longer seemed an impassable roadblock. In the process, we also learned the joy of giving as we shared our creations with others. When I suggested that we return to the textbook, she replied, "Yeah, I better. I haven't done any math in two weeks."*

A unit study encourages the use of local and often free resources. The library is a great place to start. Once that source is tapped out, it's time to turn to friends, family, and neighbors, the church library, and search for sources online.

It is not necessary to cover every detail of every subject, but instead to have a mastery of topic's basic information. Most unit studies are naturally open to application of a variety of subjects. In the cooking for math example, fractions and measuring were emphasized in the process of preparing a variety of recipes. If science had been the focus, more emphasis would have been on the chemical reactions of different ingredients.

A good unit study should include elements that cover a variety of subjects such as history, art and music; science, chemistry, biology and creation; literature, writing, grammar, spelling, punctuation and comprehension; math and phonics. There are numerous ways of incorporating these subjects including biographies and historical novels, fine art and artists, audio and video cassettes, computer software, poetry and song books, cookbooks, science experiments, theater (both live and on film), websites and games. Just as one mom uses a cookbook to teach math, you can use whatever you have at your disposal to impart knowledge to your children. The following is an example of an unplanned unit study.

> *After reading the American Girl series of books about a young girl named Kit who grew up during the Great Depression, it was all our first grader would talk about. She wanted to know everything about Kit; what would happen to her family, what she would be when she grew up, what would the rest of her life be like, would the Depression ever end, and so on. Our desire to find probable answers to these questions led us to non-fiction books about the era including biographies [history]. She read aloud and copied paragraphs from them [reading and handwriting]. We tried and compared recipes from then and now [math and history]. She contacted and interviewed people who had lived through it [communication and social skills]. She shared her knowledge with others [public speaking].*

The best way to gain and retain knowledge is to put it to practical real-life use. This book contains plenty of activities to help you do that. Each topic can be worked on as a comprehensive unit; various activities can be chosen individually or you can select a key word and run with it on your own. These key words are printed in bold type throughout the chapters and are suggestions for vocabulary assignments, spelling lists, search engines, library hunts or as a specific topic for a research project. The chapters are filled with activities to try at home as well as fun and informative things to do during your visit. There are explanations for many of the exhibits in the park and ways to relate them to your study. Home educators will be satisfied with the depth of the study even if they never visit the park, yet it is concise enough for the family who has just seven days to make it around the world (Walt Disney World) and back. The material is designed to be flexible, and used by anyone.

Now that you have a basic idea of how it all works, choose a unit and get going.

Remember to have fun and the learning will take care of itself.

Did you buy this book on the way to your vacation destination?

Are you in the car already and think it's too late to study all these areas before you get there?

Did you just get back from your trip to Walt Disney World?

Are you leaving in thirty days and think you can't possibly do all the units before you go? You are right, it's too much material to cover in that short time, and it wouldn't be much fun to try.

Don't fret!

Most of the activities can be done when you get home. Read the book, use the background information to make the experience more interesting and when you get home, start working on the units, reminding your children of everything you saw and did.

Go to Tom Sawyer island and read The adventures of Tom Sawyer. It's okay to read the book after you go instead of before.

Ride the Steamboat. Study that period in history; before you go or after you get home.

We wrote the Vacation Education Books with the idea that studying the background of the attractions, and then going to see them would make the vacation experience more meaningful and educational, but it's your family... use it the way it works for you.

Park Map

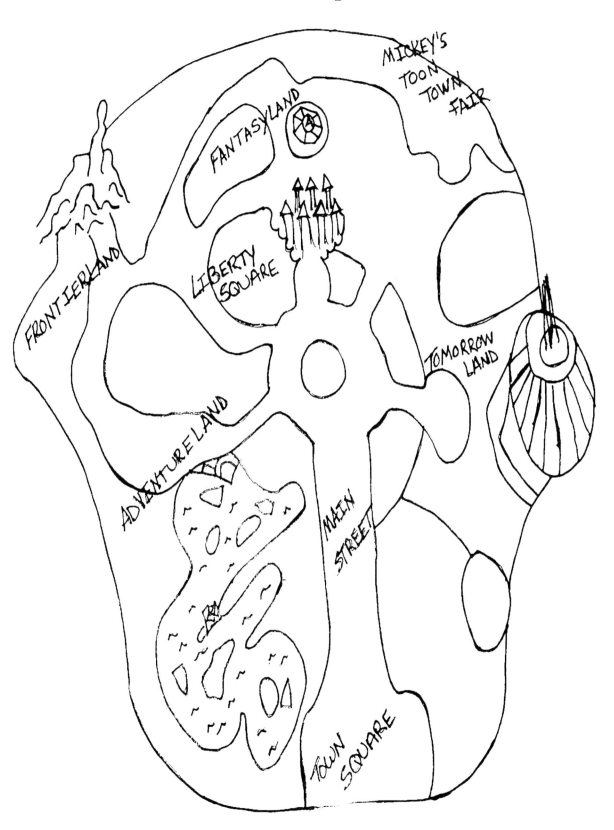

Getting Around The Park

This park is designed in a hub and spoke system, moving guests from Cinderella's castle (the hub) out to a land (a spoke) and back again to the hub. There are several books, websites and other resources that claim to have the most efficient and effective touring plan depending on your purpose. This book will guide you chronologically through the time periods covered by the attractions, but this is not the most efficient or effective way to tour the actual park. We've provided a few maps and tips for you, but we recommend The Unofficial Guide to Walt Disney World for the best touring plans.

If you are going during a busy season, having an advanced plan will be especially important. Before you go, you can put your activity cards in the order of your tour to help keep you organized throughout the day.

> *"The activity cards came in really handy. Every time we took them out, people around us would ask about them. Especially the scavenger hunts."*

FANTASYLAND
MAP

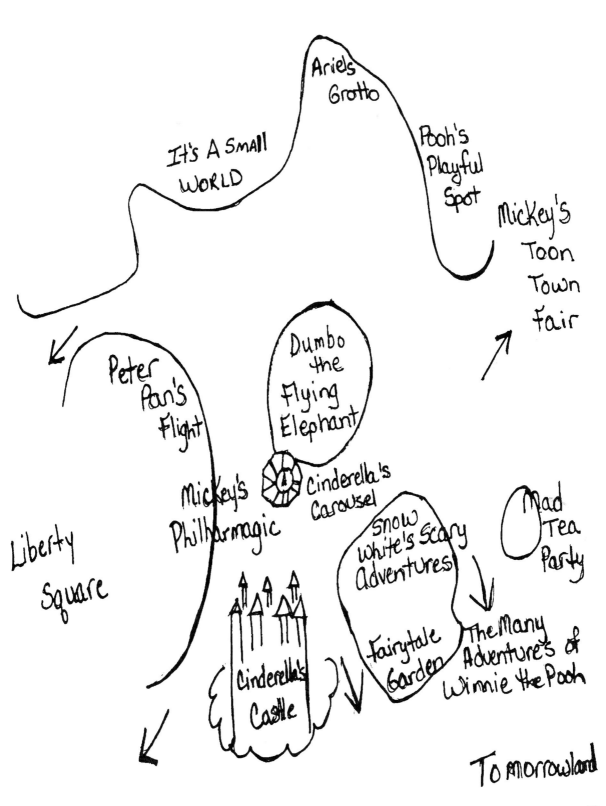

Fairy Tales, Myths and Legends

A spoiler warning is in order before you get your heart or your child's heart set on doing fairy tales, myths and legends. If you like the way that Disney presents stories, and you want to keep them that way in your mind, then you might be disappointed when you delve into the history and learn the origin of these stories.

☑ CHECK IT OUT!
Throughout the Disney movies, there seems to be a common link: it is raining in the scenes when the hero and villain are fighting. Is this always true, somewhat true, or just an occasional coincidence? Watch several of these movies, then you decide.

In preparing this study, I felt it was the most desirable for building logical thinking skills, learning to analyze objectively, developing personal opinions, and for comparing and contrasting. So, with that in mind, this study is designed with the intention of comparing the original stories to Disney's versions. This is not intended to either criticize or compliment Disney's adaptations of stories, only to learn to discern differences in literature. As I was finishing up this writing, we heard of a college professor who had done something very similar to this with her literature course. This is probably a study most applicable to high school and college age students, and adults may enjoy working on it as well. The unit is research intensive, and involves a lot of reading and writing projects.

As stories are passed from generation to generation, the telling changes, and since many of them began as oral traditions, they can be difficult to trace back to original versions. As you study each of these stories, you will be asked to analyze them for more than content, to seek out their purpose in cultures and how the changes made throughout the years affected the people who heard them. Then, look at the way Disney adapted them to meet his needs, what changes did he make? What did he keep the same? What purpose do his changes serve?

Students should be able to examine a tale from many different angles and then present what they have learned. The presentation is more important than the materials used.

Oral presentations should involve a process of research and preparation. A video camera is a great asset in being able to see ones self and judge stage presence. Nervous habits, such as hand wringing, nail biting, hair twirling, wiggling, etc should be controlled throughout the presentation. A time limit can be imposed, three to five minutes is common in school environments, but if you can keep the information interesting for longer, there are certainly careers available for proficient speakers. The length of the material is less important than the quality of the presentation.

Written presentations should reflect the best of the students writing abilities. We ask our children to write out their work by hand and then type their final draft of the material into the computer, so that they remain familiar with both communication mediums. Spelling, grammar, and sentence structure do matter as much as the content; no matter how well we tell a story, if the reader can't read it, we've offered them nothing.

For the younger set, don't worry that your study will be too advanced. Fantasyland is already attractive to them. You will have no trouble engaging them in listening to fairy tales again and again. Your younger guests will enjoy the story and attractions just as they are and the more mature guests will appreciate the challenge to see the story beneath the surface.

Park Tip: For those families with small children Fantasyland has two great areas to play.

Pooh's Playful Spot—this is a dry area with play equipment for young children and shady spots for moms and dads to rest and recharge for the rest of your day. Pooh and his friends frequently stop by.

Ariel's Grotto—this is a character greeting spot, but is also a wet area to play and cool off!

Disney has begun to plan activities and events especially for the five and under crowd. Part of this includes special concerts at Disney Studios and Magical Beginnings mornings. These special mornings allow families with children five and under to arrive and enter the park one hour early. Only Fantasyland is open, but all the rides here are available and there are characters galore, not only posing for photos and signing autographs, but leading the kids in songs and games.

"Our children were part of a group of about ten kids who got to play with Peter Pan, Wendy and Captain Hook. It was great fun!"

Cinderella's Castle

Cinderella is probably the most well known of all the Disney films. It's Cinderella's castle that marks the center of the Magic Kingdom. This fair lady's castle is the hub of the entire park. Sleeping Beauty is the princess who gave Disney his big start in full length animated films, but she is living happily in her own palace at the center of Disney Land in Anaheim, California. The castle here in the WDW Magic Kingdom stands 1890+ feet tall, and can be seen from as far as two miles away. Herb Ryman is the artist who designed this famous example of French Gothic architecture.

CHECK IT OUT! As you pass through the walkway below the castle, take some time to view the walls adorned with elaborate mosaics depicting the Cinderella story. This artistry was designed by **Dorothea Redmond**. The coat of arms that appears here belongs to the Disney family.

TRY IT! When you pass by the wishing well - go ahead, throw a few pennies - it won't make your wishes come true, but it might help someone else's since the money collected here is used to support children's charities.

DID YOU KNOW? If you point your camera at just the right angle when your looking at Cinderella's fountain, you can get the crown in the background to look like it is sitting on her head. This is a great opportunity for your budding photographer to try out her skills.

FIND OUT! Why Cinderella wears **glass** slippers? Wouldn't that be impractical? Are there versions that use other materials? There was a time that glass was not easily available and quite rare and expensive. Do clues like this help you place a version of a tale in time?

Let's find out more about this fairy tale...

DID YOU KNOW? The word Cinderella is French for Little Cinder Girl.

There are hundreds of different versions of the Cinderella story. The first known version of this story comes from China and was probably written around 860, but the most well known version was written by French author Charles Perrault.

I would challenge older students and those adept at reading and researching to find at least fifteen to compare. For younger students or families pressed for time, I would suggest five. Make a chart to compare the different titles. The more versions you are able to examine, the better your chart will turn out. Compare the versions by answering the following questions for each one.

⇒ Where does the story take place? Remember that this is a story popular around the world, so different cultures will have different versions.

⇒ What are Cindy's circumstances? Is she faced with an evil stepmother and step sisters in every version, or are there other antagonists?

⇒ Who are Cindy's allies? Disney's version gives her animal friends... what about the others?

⇒ Do all of the stories have happy endings? These are just some questions to get you started. Write down any others that you can think of before you get started, and when you're done, you will be able to analyze the stories side by side on your chart.

♦ Remember, when searching for this in your library, you will want to check both adult and children's sections, and look not only for Cinderella, but for collections of fairy tales as well.

Charles Perrault is credited with the version that has Cinderella wearing glass slippers. In 1697, glass was only being produced in Venice, and was done very expensively at that. Glass was worth more than gold; to have shoes made of glass was a sign of excessive wealth. The Grimms version would change this as by the beginning of the 1800's when they were collecting stories to publish; glass was cheap to own, but impractical for shoes; it breaks easily, you know.

There are other variations as well, such as Perraults version has the main character letting her slipper fall from her foot to the step, an intentional move to bring the Prince looking for her. What do these differences tell us about the authors and the culture in which the stories were produced?

The 'Kinder und Hausmarchen' (1812) is likely to have been the first attempt to document in writing the stories of the German people. The Grimm brothers attempted to gain these tales in the purest form possible directly from the common people of Germany. Wilhelm and Jakob Grimm are most known for the fairy tales that appear in the "Marchen". Grimms version is more violent than Disney's, but is still a beautiful story of magic and love.

FIND OUT! Locate and read each version; Perrault, Grimm and Disney. Determine which of the earlier versions most influenced the Disney version; then present your conclusion and the evidence to support it.

DID YOU KNOW?

The voice of Cinderella is Ilene Woods. **?**

Actress Helene Stanley was the live action reference for Cinderella. The movie creators would film Stanley acting out the part and then use this film to copy to animation, so that the characters movements would be as realistic as possible. Viewers would instinctively notice an awkward or inappropriate movement and it would take away from the flow of the story. Stanley was also used in the creation of Princess Aurora (Sleeping Beauty) and Anita Radcliff (101 Dalmations).

CHECK IT OUT! Watch all three movies. Are their movements and postures the same or not? Keep in mind that the actress would have actually played the parts of these characters and been filmed. Animators would then create the characters from the film footage. So, it is almost as though the same actress played all three parts with different costumes on. Can you tell?

Moms and Dads, you may want to present the assignment to your children and have them make their observations prior to telling them that it was the same actress or how the process works, and see if they can tell on their own. Have them write down their observations as they watch the films. You may have to mute the sound in order to really focus on just the movements of the characters.

Here are some other suggestions for discussion questions.

⇒ Grimm does not mention a deadline of midnight, but instead has Cinderella trying to hide her own identity and rushing off in order to return home before her sisters and step-mother.

⇒ Grimms' version has several days of festivities and courtship, while Disney's version relies on love at first sight. What does this say about the corresponding cultures?

⇒ As you read each version, consider the culture it was written in and the place in time. What can we learn from the popular stories of a culture?

What's Inside?

Everyone always wants to know... What is the castle like on the inside? Is it all just make believe ? A façade? Or is it just as magical on the other side of those walls?

Inside the castle are a few specialty shops like the Bibbity Bobbity Boutique where little boys and girls can be transformed into princesses and pirates. There is also Cinderella's Royal Table restaurant (advanced reservations required). The Disney family coat of arms can be seen here; it is a field of white with three lions.

A long standing rumor was that there was an apartment, or at least an office designed and built personally for Walt in the upper rooms of the castle. In an effort to please their guests, Disney has made this dream come true. There is a suite in the castle that can not be reserved or rented, but is always free... as part of Disney's year of a million dreams program, they are giving away a million dreams, and one of those is to spend the night in Cinderella's Castle. Every day in the Magic Kingdom, some family some where in the park is randomly chosen to be the dream winners, and they get to spend that night in the castle. A dream come true.

I read Cinderella by...

My Favorite Part of the Story is

The Little Mermaid
Attraction: ARIEL's Grotto

This story can be traced back to Italian author Giovanni Straparalo, and was probably written around 1550. It is also credited to Hans Christian Andersen. But, the version used in the movie and the Broadway play is an adaptation of Andersen's tale written by Roger Allers.

FIND OUT! What changes did Allers make to the storyline as he prepared it for Disney audiences? You will have to find a copy of the Andersen version written all the way back in 1836, and compare it to the 1989 film version.

Alan Menken and Howard Ashman were the song writing team for this film, and many others. If you can think of a film where the story was pretty much carried by the musical soundtrack (like The Little Mermaid or Beauty and the Beast), these two probably had something to do with that.

FIND OUT! What other movies contain music by Menken and Ashman? What other movie scripts did Allers work on? Write them here and see if they have any others in common.

CHECK IT OUT! If you happen to see Ariel at her Grotto, and then again at the Princess' Royal Feast, you will have two autographs that are similar but not identical. This would be true of any character whose autograph you happen to get twice. Even though the actors are trained to write each signature a certain way, there are distinct differences in peoples handwriting. Use this comparison to begin a study of the elements that an expert analyst would look for in determining the authenticity of documents.

DID YOU KNOW? Ariels sisters names are Aquata, Andrina, Arista, Atlina, Adella, and **?**

I read The Little Mermaid by:

My favorite part of this story is:

BEAUTY and the BEAST
Attraction: Belle's Storytime

VOCABULARY

Barbie & the Nutcracker

Sherri Stoner

Paige O'Hara

Howard Ashman

Madame De Villeneuve

Giovanni Straparalo

ancient mythology

Literary clubs

Christian courtship

Aesop

 TRY IT! IN THE PARK! You can see Belle in Fantasyland if you catch a scheduled story time with her. This is a fitting activity for Belle, as in the Disney version of the story, she is a bit of a bookworm. Belle brings alive the magic of her movie through her story telling. Belle's Garden is small so plan to get there early to insure seating. Someone in your group may be asked to dress up and participate in the story, so bring your camera. After the story, Belle usually stays around to talk with guests and sign autographs as well as pose for pictures.

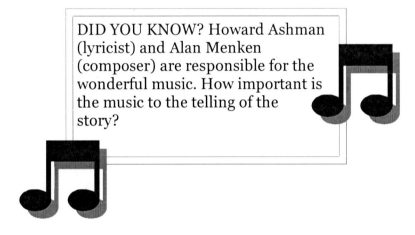

DID YOU KNOW? Howard Ashman (lyricist) and Alan Menken (composer) are responsible for the wonderful music. How important is the music to the telling of the story?

CHECK IT OUT! Watch the film on mute, so you can still read the lines, but can't hear the music. Does it have an affect on the way the story makes you feel?

TRY IT! Watch the movie before you leave for the trip. It premiered on November 22, 1991, and should be easy to find in your local video rental store or maybe at your local library. It is common in animation of realistic humans to use actual people for reference. In **Barbie and the Nutcracker,** the animators filmed world class ballerinas to use as a guide for the movements of the dancers. Disney chose actress **Sherri Stoner** for the character of Belle, while her voice is that of actress **Paige O'Hara.** In the credits you will notice that an animator is given credit for each of the characters. Sometimes, the animators didn't even see each other but were able to coordinate scenes by sending drawings back and forth.

CHECK IT OUT! Read the book(s): The original story was written in 1740 by Madame De Villeneuve, but may have been adapted from a 'Beauty' character created by Italian author Giovanni Straparalo, and even he may have gotten it from as far back as ancient mythology. It truly is a tale as old as time, but how old? See if you can find out.

 TRY IT! This is a great opportunity to create a timeline. See how many versions you can track down, and make a timeline showing their authors and publication dates.

Suggested Reading List

'Beauty and the Beast' Jan Brett

'The Dragon Prince: A Chinese Beauty and the Beast Tale' Laurence Yep

To maintain the "magic" while you are in the park, we suggest waiting until you get home to do a literary comparison with young children. However, we do think that by learning similarities and differences, they are learning that things are not always as we first think they are.

You can search for the word Beauty in the title section of your library and will likely find several renditions of this age-old tale.

Just as an example, here is a sampling of titles available from Amazon.
Under the title of Beauty and the Beast, there are books by the following authors:
Max Eilenberg
M. Mayer
Madame D'Aulroy
Samantha Easton
Nancy Willard
Geraldine McCaughrean
Carol Heyer
The same basic story under other titles:
Lady and The Lion by Jacqueline K. Ogburn
Cupid and Psyche by M. Charlotte Craft
The Great Smelly, Slobbery, Small tooth dog: A folktale from Great Britain by Margaret Read MacDonald
The Scarlet Flower: A Russian Folk Tale by S.T. Aksakov
Snowbear Whittington: An Appalachian Beauty and the Beast by William H. Hooks

This is not an exhaustive list.

TRY IT! Start a literary club, your library probably has a room you can meet in and will help you advertise. Discuss the differences in the versions you've read. Here are some discussions questions to use with your group, or to research on your own. There is space available for you to write your answers or take notes.

*In many older versions, the Beast demanded that the father bring him his daughter in trade for stealing the rose. In Disney's version, Belle ventures out in search of her father and offers herself in trade. What does each represent about the role of women in the corresponding cultures?

*Belle and the Beast spend many months getting to know each other, which is different from many fairy tale characters like Cinderella and Snow White, who fall in love upon meeting their prince charming. Research information on Christian Courtship, and compare it to dating rituals of today. What are the similarities and differences? How do you think the differences would affect their marriages if these were actual relationships of real people?

* Aesops fables always end with "And the moral of the story is…" If Aesop had written Beauty and the Beast, what do you think the moral of the story would be? Perhaps beauty is in the eye of the beholder; beauty is only skin deep; what someone is like inside is more important than how they look on the outside, etc.

*This story has been called the greatest love story of all time. Why do you think that is? Do you agree or disagree? Defend your answer.

*From the beginning of the story to the end, Belle and the Beast both go through changes in their demeanor and perspective, what are they? What other changes do you notice?

EPCOT! If Epcot is on your travel itinerary, be sure to pick up a copy of Vacation Education destination Epcot. Visit France in the World Showcase as this is the home of Belle, and you may even find her here, available for photo opportunities and autographs. There is a unit study on France in the Epcot guide, and it would complement this study of Fairy Tales quite well. Beauty of the Beast could lead to discussions of French culture and history, or vice versa.

THIS IS A LINK TO THE STUDIOS!

If you happen to include Disney MGM Studios theme park in your travel plans, be sure to see Beauty and the Beast live on stage. This is a Broadway style and Broadway caliber show.

IN PARK TIP: The Theater of the Stars is shaded, but is not air-conditioned, so morning shows might be more comfortable.

This 20+ minute show is preceded by an entertaining pre-show. The pre-show is in no way related to the headliner, but provides a distraction for those who arrive 30 minutes early to insure seating (which is recommended, especially during high attendance dates).

When studying this story's history, the live production does not add much to your research as it is only an abridged version of the Disney film. However, Disney's live shows are very well done, and an excellent introduction to live theater, especially if you do not live close enough to attend a show on Broadway (or can't afford the ticket prices). Disney shows, like Beauty and the Beast are included in your park admission, so see as many as you like.

If you were not familiar with the story, would this stage show be easy enough to follow (even though it is very condensed, showing just highlights from the movie)?

What are the integral plot points that are used in this stage production to tell the story in as short a time as possible?

In the first scene at the castle, there are two gargoyles at the foot of the stair. When the spell is broken, these become golden cherubs. What other subtle but important changes do you notice? What affect would it have on the show if these details were neglected?

See the MGM Link in Theater and Drama for more on this topic!

I read Beauty and the Beast by...

This is my favorite part of the story...

_____

- -
_____
_____
- -
_____
_____
- -
_____
_____
- -
_____
_____
- -
_____
_____
- -
_____

Cinderella's Carousel

This is a neat place to pause and mention the history of Walt Disney and his world. Walt frequently visited the Griffith Park carousel with his daughters. They would go round and round while he watched from a nearby bench. It was here that he first began to imagine a place where parents and children could enjoy the rides together. This is a fundamental part of what keeps generations of Disney guests coming back for more. There are very few attractions that have limitations of height, size or age. Everyone can join in the fun!

 TRY IT! Every creature on this carousel is unique. Can you find the special horse that Cinderella herself would ride? Hint: It's the one with the golden ribbon on its tail.

Baby Tip: I wore my one year old in a backpack carrier all week at every park. I was able to ride almost everything without even taking him off. This made it possible for our family to stay together all day instead of someone sitting out with the baby.

CHECK IT OUT! Try to identify the scenes from the movie Cinderella that have been hand painted on the ceiling.

 DID YOU KNOW? This carousel wasn't built for Disney, it was originally built in 1917 for a New Jersey amusement park. Walt had it refurbished and artists hand painted scenes from Cinderella onto the canopy.

Park Tip: Behind the carousel is one of the best spots to view the fireworks 'Fantasy in the Sky'.

The Sword and The Stone

The king has died, there is no obvious heir to the throne. Merlin the magician has placed a sword into a stone, and cast a spell such that only the chosen heir could pull the sword from the stone. Who could it be? Everyone wants it, everyone will try to pull the sword from the stone.

 Photo Opportunity: Try to pull the sword out of the stone.

Vocabulary List
Merlin, the magician
T.H. White
Bill Peet
Screenplay
Knight
Squire
England
John the Baptist
Archimedes

The story comes from a novel by T.H. White. But, Bill Peet is the author of the storyline or screenplay that Disney used for the making of the 1963 film.

The in park connection to the storyline is limited to the sword in the stone and plaque at Cinderella's Carousel.

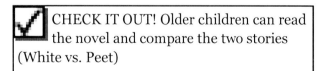 CHECK IT OUT! Older children can read the novel and compare the two stories (White vs. Peet)

There are several elements in the film that merit discussion. We never allow our children to view films unsupervised (unless we've previewed them). At our house movie night is a special event, something we do as a family with pop, pizza, popcorn; the works. Here are some suggestions for conversation starters. We hope that you will use these as a guide and start thinking of your family's entertainment as an opportunity to grow together.

- In the movie, England needs a king, just like Israel needed a Savior. From this perspective, how is Merlin's anticipation of the king to come similar to John the Baptist's expectation of Christ's coming? Merlin tells Archimedes that he must prepare for someone coming; he doesn't know exactly when he'll come, but it could be any day now. (Luke 3:3-6, Luke 3:16-17)

- At the beginning of the movie, during the narration, a light shines down from heaven onto the place where the sword is placed into the stone. How is this similar to the star that shined the way for the Wise Men? In both cases, the light shows the place where the king/Savior will be revealed. (Matthew 3:13-17)

- There are elements of magic integral to the telling of this story. Does this make it a fairy tale? There are examples in Scripture of magic. In Exodus, Pharoah's magicians are able to use their magical powers to copy the plagues of God. Where else does scripture discuss magic? What does scripture tell us about magic? (Use a Concordance to look up verses about magic, magicians, witches, and witchcraft)

- The promise from heaven (in the movie) is that someone will come and pull out the sword, and that will be a sign for all to see that he is the next king. What sign did God use to show that David was meant to be the next king? (Ist Samuel 16:1-13)

- Many men tried to pull the sword from the stone. The people believed that pulling the sword from the stone took great strength, physical strength and therefore the next king would have to be an extremely strong man. What were some of the misconceptions that the Jews had about who the Savior would be?

- No one was able to pull the sword out right away although many had tried; none of them was the true heir to the throne and soon the promise of a king was forgotten by many, and thorns grew over the sword. From the time of Noah, when everyone on earth (all eight of them) believed wholeheartedly in God and His promises until the time of Jesus' life on earth, what happened to the people's faith in that promise?

- In the movie, there is a wolf who keeps coming after Arthur, and each time Arthur narrowly escapes. What does the wolf represent in scripture? (See Genesis 49:27, Ezekiel 22:27, Matthew 7:15)

- Arthur is the heir to the kingdom because of who his father was, but he spent the first twelve years of his life being raised by a foster father. Jesus also had a surrogate father, Joseph, and He also gains his position because of who is Father is. Where in scripture can you learn about the inheritance that you will receive because of who your Father is?

- The tournament for kingship shows that the people of England had turned from God's promises and sought for themselves their own way of selecting a king. What examples can you think of where God's people turned from His promises and tried to do things their own way?

- In the end, when Arthur pulls the sword from the stone, the crowd mocks him and even shouts sarcastically, "He's a young Samson." Again, this shows the people's misguided ideas about who the king was supposed to be. But, the light from heaven shines down on him to show that he is the chosen one. Read together the scripture where the Holy Spirit comes down on Jesus to show that He is God's chosen one. (Matthew 3: 13-17)

DID YOU KNOW? This production is not a musical as many of the more recent films have been, like Beauty and the Beast or The Little Mermaid (both films that were carried by their phenomenal soundtracks). The Sword and The Stone does have a few musical numbers.

"Our favorite song from this movie was the Magnificent Marvelous Mad Madam Mim."

Jesus was tempted three times (Matthew 4:1-11). Arthur was tested by Merlin three times as well. Each time he was turned into a different animal, and faced a different element of danger. Use this space to write down the three animals that he was turned into and the lessons that he was supposed to learn from each.

1.

2.

3.

"This is my favorite line [from this film], "That love business is a powerful thing... the greatest force on earth." Merlin, the magician.

DUMBO
Attraction: Dumbo, the Flying Elephant

This ride is based on the 1941 film , and is one of the most popular rides in this park, or at least it seems that way as the wait is always outrageous. Be prepared for long lines if your children insist on riding this .

 Photo Opportunity: There is a ride car off to the side if you didn't get a good shot of your kids on the ride .

Vocabulary List
Helen Aberson
Roll-A-Book
Joe Grant
A-film
Market saturation
Re-releases
remastered

While this story does fit some of the fairy tale elements, and it certainly fits into the category of folk tales; the original story is not much older than the film. Disney had just finished Pinnochio when he discovered a story published by a company called Roll-A-Book. Helen A. Mayer, an author of children's stories from Syracuse New York was contacted, Walt Disney quickly bought the rights to the story and Joe Grant, a Disney writer, adapted the story for the screen. From a small press edition (less than one thousand copies were published initially) in 1939, to the 1941 movie and on to the fame it claims today.

Dumbo opened in theaters on October 23rd, 1941, as a 64 minute film. Walt had insisted, amongst objections that it be released as an A-film. It was made for half the cost of Snow White, and was the only other Disney film at the time to show a profit.

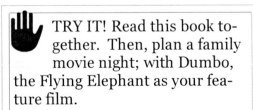 TRY IT! Read this book together. Then, plan a family movie night; with Dumbo, the Flying Elephant as your feature film.

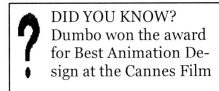
 CHECK IT OUT! The musical direction for this film
was provided by Frank Churchill and Oliver Wallace.

Dumbo continued to be a family favorite throughout the decades as well as financially lucrative for Disney Co., despite being interrupted by the start of WWII. It was re-released in theaters in 1949, giving audiences another chance to support it. Then, in case anyone missed it, again in 1959, 1972, and 1976.

As if that wasn't market saturation enough, Dumbo holds the honor of being the first Disney feature film to be released on home video. The VHS version hit store shelves in 1981.

Then, Disney went a little overboard (maybe?) with the whole re-releasing strategy, but that and limited edition releases seem to do quite well for them financially. Dumbo came out in 1985 (as a Disney Classic), 1986 (as a remastered version of the original), 1989 (remastered again), 1991 (remastered yet again, this time as a Classic), 1994 (Masterpiece Edition), 2001 (60th anniversary edition) and 2006 (Big Top Edition) on DVD. I suspect we have yet to see the end.

CHECK IT OUT! At 64 minutes, this is the shortest of all of Disney's animated feature films. From a book published in 1939 to a theater release in 1941, it's also one of the fastest ever

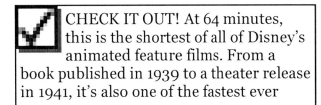 DID YOU KNOW? Aberson continued to write children's stories until her death in 1999, but Dumbo was the only one ever published.

Q? Who is the voice of Dumbo?

A: No one. He doesn't have any lines.

ALICE in Wonderland
Attraction: Mad Hatter's Tea Party

The intention of this crazy spinning ride is to take guests on a trip into Wonderland with Alice as she tries to make sense of the Mad Hatters ramblings.

Vocabulary List

Lewis Carroll

Charles Lutwidge Dodgeson

John Tenniel

anthropomorphic

FIND OUT! How many other writings by Lewis Carroll can you find? Name them here:

? DID YOU KNOW? The illustrations for the book were done by **John Tenniel.**

This story was originally the work of Lewis Carroll, which is a pen name for Reverend Charles Lutwidge Dodgeson. In 1862, Dodgeson told a story to his friends three daughters as a way to pass the time. They loved it so much, he wrote it down. Over the next three years, he added many details to the tale of 'Alice's Adventures in Wonderland', and then had it published. Seven years later, he followed it with a sequel, 'Through the Looking Glass and What Alice Found There.'

Although the books brought great fame to the name Lewis Carroll; Dodgeson was a shy and reserved man who went to great lengths to hide his identity. Those he knew were portrayed rather obviously in the stories though. We hear a tale of three sisters from the Dormouse. They are named for the three young ladies that he first wrote the story for. Elsie refers to Lorina Charlotte, whose initials are L.C. Tillie was a nickname for Edith, and Lacie is an anagram for Alice. It's not to much of a stretch to think that Dodgeson was speaking of Lorina, Alice and Edith.

Some of the characters you will meet in this charming book are, of course, Alice, a young girl who chases a rabbit into its rabbit hole. The white rabbit who she is chasing leads her into a land of wonders, a land filled with unusual and unexpected surprises. There is of course, the Mad Hatter, who this attraction is named after. Read about Alice's visit to his tea party and this ride will make perfect sense.

CHECK IT OUT! This writing is a classic example of English nonsense literature.

FIND OUT! Dodgeson makes several references to many traditional English poems of his time. Can you identify

 CHECK IT OUT! The first "Alice" movie was produced by Cecil M. Hepworth in 1903.

 DID YOU KNOW? There have been more than a dozen adaptations since then, including Disney's animated version in 1951 which combined stories from both of Carroll's books.

Tim Burton will release yet another adaptation of Carroll's stories in 2008.

TRY IT! & SHARE IT! Memorize your favorite poem and recite it for others. Maybe at a Fine Arts Festival or talent show.

CHECK IT OUT! The Mad Tea Party happens in Chapter 7.

DID YOU KNOW? This title has never been out of print! Since 1865!

In 1998, a copy of that first printing in 1865 was auctioned for $1.5 million!

Choose your favorite character
Draw it here:

SNOW WHITE
Attraction: Snow White's Scary Adventures

VOCABULARY

Snow White

Full length feature

Gross sales

Animated film

Blockbuster

Dwarf

adjective

✓ CHECK IT OUT! Walt Disney is famous for putting out this first full length animated film, when critics said no one would watch a ninety minute cartoon. What did they know? The movie was released on December 21, 1937, and received gross sales of $8 million. That might not seem like much compared to todays movies, but that's a whole lot of ten cent tickets. See how fast you can name three or more animated films that have been recent blockbusters. Write them here.

If you have never seen this film, and are planning to watch it with your family, be forewarned that this is a scary movie. Even by todays standards with constantly advancing technology, this story is intense with some very frightening elements. There is the innocence of Snow White (this name represents the most perfectly innocent as it brings forth the image of Christs blood washing us as white as snow, perfectly clean before God). The opposite of pure goodness has to be pure evil, and this is how the witch is portrayed, and she is scary.

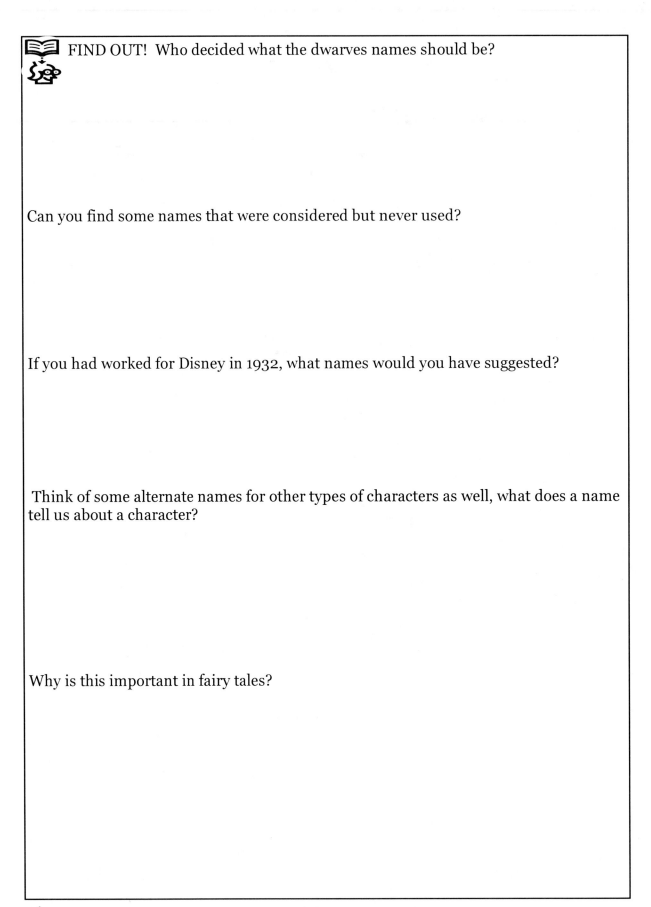

FIND OUT! Who decided what the dwarves names should be?

Can you find some names that were considered but never used?

If you had worked for Disney in 1932, what names would you have suggested?

Think of some alternate names for other types of characters as well, what does a name tell us about a character?

Why is this important in fairy tales?

DID YOU KNOW? In the first scene of Snow White's Adventures, she is sitting on the stairs wearing wooden shoes. Although we normally associate wooden shoes with the Dutch, they are also a common form of footwear amidst German history. Villagers in rural Germany still wore wooden shoes for their daily activities, saving the more expensive leather shoes for church, well into the 1960's.

Words Used to Describe Characters

Adjectives are important to writing, whether for books, or for screenplays and films. Disney incorporated many opposing adjective to set up a feel for the personalities of the two main characters. Compare and discuss these lists of words that are used to describe the characters of the Queen and Snow White.

Snow White	Queen
Fair	Vain
Beauty	Wicked
Young	Cruel
	Witch
	Jealous

TRY IT! Now, take a look at the animation. While the writers are responsible for using words to tell the story, and adjectives are important, the animators must also tell a story through pictures. What are some of the characteristics drawn on the characters that help you to see their personality? Some examples are the Queen scowls while Snow White is almost always drawn smiling; and vultures watch and wait for death around the Queen, and from the beginning of the story, Snow White is often surrounded by doves and other small friendly woodland animals. What other examples can you find? Use additional paper if necessary.

While the animation is what Walt is famous for, it takes a good story to captivate an audience. This story is a perfect example of classic Disney style... a world that is not void of evil, but a world in which good always overcomes evil. Can you find some of the storyline details that make this point? Here are some of the discussion questions that are family used. Can you think of some more?

**The Queen wants Snow White's heart cut out. A person's life is in their heart, but it is also the place where the Holy Spirit resides. To have a person's heart is to have their mind and soul as well. What do you think is the Queen's underlying motivation for wanting Snow White's heart in her possession?

**Snow White's behavior shows her as naïve, innocent, and sweet as she cares for the small woodland animals. She wins over the huntsman and he is unable to follow through with murdering her. She is also very maternal in her relationship to the animals and the dwarves, like a little girl who lovingly takes care of her dolls. Identify some of her behaviors that are childlike, and some that are more maternal and mature.

**Compare the musical and drawing elements as the movie switches from a dark scene to a lighter scene and back again. For example, when Snow White is running for her life, fear is represented by the imaginary creatures she sees in the trees in the dark, but mostly in the dark music that accompanies this scene. Contrast this with the scene that immediately follows, the next morning, when the forest is bright and the animals are her friends. What other examples do you see of this contrast between dark and light, good and evil?

**What part does music play in evoking the emotions of these scenes?

 TRY IT! IN THE PARK! In the movie, the credits list several animators. Can you find a tribute to any of these animators on the windows of Main Street?

**Each dwarf has a distinct name and personality. What did the animators do in their drawings to help you identify which is which without name tags? What features are drawn on each one that represents his personality? It can be hard to remember all their names, so I've listed them for you.

**Dopey

**Grumpy

**Bashful

**Sleepy

**Doc

**Sneezy

**Happy

**There are elements of Christian faith represented throughout the story, such as Snow White saying her bedtime prayers and the Queen's downward spiral as she turns to spells and black magic to get her way. What others can you identify?

Disney animators are famous for their humorous gags. These can be found throughout the movie. Here are some of our favorites, List yours below.

"Grumpy gets his nose stuck in a tree because he gets dizzy after Snow White kisses him on the head."

"The turtle's belly gets used as a washboard."

"Pretty much everything Dopey does."

It's a Small World
Fairy Tale? Myth? Legend?

Vocabulary

Sherman brothers

World's Fair

Joyce Carlson

Culture

Dollmaker

Technology

canal

The cute little dancing dolls of this exhibit had their debut performance at the 1964-65 New York World's Fair. At the time, the technology for this ride was the first of its kind. No one had seen anything like it. A boat floating through a canal; it was a ride like no other. The ride itself was quieter than most other rides. The dolls went from the World's Fair to Disneyland and were copied for Walt Disney World in 1971.

DID YOU KNOW? Joyce Carlson was the doll maker for this exhibit and many others. Look for the window dedicated to her on Main Street.

DID YOU KNOW? The Sherman Brothers wrote the song "It's a Small World" and the theme song for the Carousel of Progress? They also wrote music for the movie Mary Poppins.

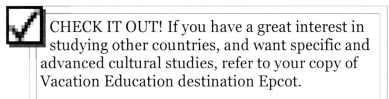
CHECK IT OUT! If you have a great interest in studying other countries, and want specific and advanced cultural studies, refer to your copy of Vacation Education destination Epcot.

 TRY IT! Try to identify each area of the world that is represented.

What are the clues that help you determine this?

Are there obvious cultural elements, like skin tone and clothing that help you?

What about the scenery?

The activities that the characters are participating in?

What do these design elements tell you about the culture and its location in the world?

TIP: Before you arrive, spend some time doing a world study that includes weather patterns (this often determines the style of dress for a society). Studying cultures around the world will help you with this activity. Use your library and look at pictures from around the world and even younger children can work on matching what they see in the attraction with what they remember from the books.

The Many Adventures of Winnie the Pooh
Attraction of the same name

This space used to belong to Mr. Toad and housed his Wild Ride (one of Walt's original attractions). The designers even included an explanation for the change. During the ride, if you look at the wall of Owl's house; you will see Toad passing the land deed over to Owl. Those Imagineers think of everything.

The hunny pot vehicles take you on a journey through scenes from the stories of adventure featuring Winnie the Pooh and his friends. This is an attraction that everyone can participate in. There are no seat belts and the ride is pretty smooth except for one area where you bounce along with Tigger.

? DID YOU KNOW? This book series was created by A.A. Milne as a gift for his son Christopher Robin?

 CHECK IT OUT! Take a break in the one hundred acre play area.

Milne was a writer and poet of some fame long before he created the Winnie the Pooh stories. The characters are based on the stuffed animal friends of his only son Christopher Robin.

The illustrations were done by E.H. Shepard, and were based on his own son's stuffed animals.

These special stories of a Pooh bear and his adventures were a delight to children and parents alike all over the world. They became so famous that people forgot about the other writings of Milne.

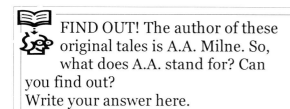 FIND OUT! The author of these original tales is A.A. Milne. So, what does A.A. stand for? Can you find out?
Write your answer here.

? DID YOU KNOW? The story <u>Toad of Toad Hall</u> was also written by Milne. It was based on an original work by Kenneth Grahame's <u>The Wind in the Willows.</u>

CHECK IT OUT! Borrow both of these tales from the library to compare. How true to Grahame's story did Milne's version stay?

Milne was an English author, trained by teachers like H.G. Wells at the Henley House School where his father was the headmaster.

Milne worked as a contributor and eventually assistant editor for Punch, a British humor magazine.

After Milne's death, Disney purchased the rights to Winnie the Pooh and friends from his widow. Royalties continued to be paid to the Royal Literary Fund who Milne had left a percentage of ownership to. Reverend David Williams set up the Royal Literary Fund in 1790 to assist British writers financially.

 CHECK IT OUT! Milne's faith is not obvious in his children's stories featuring Pooh Bear and Friends, but he did present the pubic with his opinions on matters of religion in the book "The Norman Church" (1948) Find it at your library.

CHECK IT OUT! A.A. Milne published many works, see how many you can find. Amazon has more than 80 titles listed. See how many of these you can find at your local library. Compare these writings to the Pooh series that you are familiar with.

Peter Pan
Peter Pan's Flight

Peter Pan's Flight takes you on a trip over the rooftops of London. Just pass the second star on the right and straight on until morning to reach Neverland. The theme song here is "you can fly, you can fly, you can fly". Join other guests as you follow the path that Peter took Wendy, Michael and John on.

The character of Peter Pan was created by novelist and playwright J.M. Barrie . The name Peter came from the son of one of Barrie's closest friends. Pan is the name of a mischievous Greek god of the woodlands. He was first introduced to the public in 1902 as a character in the novel <u>The Little White Bird.</u> This story is available online as a free downloadable ebook (try books.google.com).

In 1904, Peter Pan was given the honor of appearing as the main character in a theatrical play called The Boy Who Wouldn't Grow Up. It was first performed at the Duke of York's Theater on December 27, 1904. He later put the story in novel form and published the book <u>Peter Pan and Wendy</u> in 1911.

Vocabulary List

Peter Pan

J.M. Barrie

The Little White Bird

The Boy Who Wouldn't Grow Up

Duke of York's Theater

Peter Pan and Wendy

Neverland

 FIND OUT! The play, the novel and the 1953 Disney movie are not exactly the same. Locate a copy of each and compare them.

The Disney film 'Return To Neverland' is based upon one element that exists in Barrie's novel, but not in the play. After Wendy returns home, Peter promises to return for her in a year for another visit to Neverland. This movie presents an idea of what happens when Peter does actually return to Wendy's home... twenty years later.

The film Peter Pan begins with a narrator introducing the characters of the Darling family; including Wendy, of course, the eldest child and only daughter of Mr. and Mrs. Darling. She is the storyteller of the family, engaging her younger brothers in the tales she weaves. They are so engrossed in her fantasies that they play out the characters she has provided their imaginations.

"Wouldn't it be grand if we all could go on adventures in our pajamas!"

The story begins at the home of the Darling family in London. As Peter first meets Wendy, Tink is watching from inside the bureau drawer.

Tinkerbell is fierce with jealousy over Wendy, and it appears that the mermaids are too. Captain Hook uses this jealousy against her.

"One of my all time favorite movie lines is 'A jealous female can be tricked into anything.' A token of wisdom from Captain Hook."

SHARE IT! Are there times when you have been jealous of someone because they had something you wanted?

How did you handle those feelings?

Could you have done things differently?

Do you think there could have been a different outcome?

Great Co-op Activity!

 TRY IT! Write a play of your own based on you, your neighborhood friends and an imaginary place that you can all go. Do it just for fun, or get some friends together and try it out. Put on a show for the parents in your neighborhood.

 TRY IT! At the Magic Kingdom, take a walk through Tinkerbell's Treasures shop and see if you can find her there. One of the places she likes to hide is in the bureau drawer, so be sure to check there.

 SHARE IT! When the movie is over, share with each other your favorite part of the film.

"I had a white rat once... said one lost boy to another. "That's no mother!" said another in return. This sends my four year old into fits of giggles. He likes to climb into my lap and listen to Wendy sing. When his laughter is under control, he looks at me and mimics, "A rat... that's no mother!" And the giggle fit begins again.

☑ CHECK IT OUT! There is a cross where Tinkerbell lays after sacrificing herself to save Peter from the bomb. Use this opportunity to say, 'That reminds me of the sacrifice that Jesus made for us.' Both sacrifices were made out of love for another.

Peter fights Captain Hook at the end of the movie, and he agrees not to fly away. He keeps his word. Wendy's tales of Peter Pan portray him as brave and daring, adventurous and mysterious, a true boy, but not deceitful or dishonest. Hook is most assuredly the bad guy throughout the story and yet he still is the representation of an innocent child's idea of evil.

"Peter Pan reminds me of my six year old son, sometimes no matter how serious I try to be, he can't help but be playful."

Mickey's Philharmagic
Fairy Tale? Myth? Legend?

"Our daughter [8] had never been to a 3-D film before, and the first one we did was 'Bugs Life' [at the Animal Kingdom]. After that, she didn't enjoy any of them; she was convinced that things would come out of the seats and floor if she put her glasses on. This one would have been great if we'd done it first. It is tame and magical."

It opened in 2003, so if it's been a few years since you've been here, check out this show. This is a good first 3-D movie experience for the younger guests in your group, or the more timid.

The story line here is a familiar one for some of us older Disney fans. Mickey is wearing his sorcerer's hat. He's apparently earned it since 1941 when he starred in Fantasia as the sorcerer's apprentice and goofed up all sorts of things. Well, now Mickey is the master sorcerer as well as the musical conductor for the orchestra. But, when Mickey sets down his sorcerer's cap, Donald Duck comes along and seeing that no one is watching (except the entire audience of course). He decides to try it out for himself, and gets into more than a few messes because of it.

THINK ABOUT IT! After watching Donald bumble through his adventures trying to return an item that he had stolen, take this opportunity to talk about some real life examples of the trouble that is caused when ever someone does something dishonest.

VIEWING TIP: "Our kid always want to sit in the front row, but we've found this type of production is best seen from the middle or back. The 'effect' is not as effective in the first few rows."

So, is it a fairy tale, a myth or a legend? Culturally, these terms are often used interchangeably. So, what is the difference between a fairy tale, a myth and a legend? What about folk tales? Are they the same thing? Where do they fit in? FIND OUT!

Merriam Webster defines a fairy tale as: "1a: a story (as for children) involving fantastical forces and beings (as fairies, wizards and goblins) - called also fairy story. 1b: a story in which improbable events lead to a happy ending. The elements of a fairy tale tend to be set in a 'once upon a time' rather than an actual historical era. It is, of course, a work of fiction, presumed to be based on no actual historical events. They can be traced back as far as 1300 B.C. in written form, but were likely passed down orally for generations before that.

A fairy tale can have fairies in it, but they are not a necessary element. The term fairy tale has more to do with the existence of fantastical elements in the story rather than the existence of any particular type of character. We usually think of these stories as for children, but they were actually a form of adult entertainment until the 19th century when they became associated more with children's stories. These tales have changed over the years, as many stories do when passed from place to place and author to author.

So, how does a myth compare to a fairy tale? How do you tell which is which? A myth by definition (from Dictionary.com): "a traditional or legendary story, usually concerning some being or hero or event, with or without a determinable bases of fact or a natural explanation, especially one that is concerned with deities or demigods and explains some practice, rite, or phenomenon of nature."

A myth is quite often a story that is believed to have a basis in fact by many of the people in the culture that the story comes from. While these are also past down from generation to generation, they differ from fairy tales primarily because fairy tales are generally accepted as being completely made up.

Legends tend to be even more grounded in historical fact. At the very least, legends maintain an aura of possibility; it could have happened. In the originating culture, citizens will claim vehemently that the events actually happened.

SHARE IT! Locate and read several types of stories, then put in your own words the defining elements of fairy tales, myths and legends.

TRY IT! Be a literary historian. Read more than one version of a tale, so you can compare them. Tales are placed in history based on the elements in the story. Try to figure out which version came first. Defend your answer.

Topping Off The Tales

When you've finished your studies on each of the individual tales, here are some activities that will help you keep your mind fresh, and help you to top off the fairy tales, myths and legends by using what you've learned so far.

 TRY IT! What are the elements of a good fairy tale? Use these to create your own.

 SHARE IT! Read your favorite fairy tale on to a cassette tape or CD to give as a gift to a child who is just learning to read. Make sure to 'beep' when it is time to turn the page. Give both the book and the recording together as a gift.

 SHARE IT! Organize a community service project. Be a reader for a senior center or for the blind. Read to them their favorite fairy tales.

CHECK IT OUT! There are many more tales than the ones showcased by Disney. Read folk tales from around the world, especially ones that haven't been made into a movie yet. Hypothesize what elements are required to attract a movie producing company like Disney. Predict what folk tales will be make into movies in the next ten years.

SHARE IT! Choose a favorite character, prince, princess or villain and write a journal entry about a typical day in the life of your character.

TRY IT! Make puppets of the characters with felt and ribbons, or simply draw them on paper lunch bags. Put on a puppet show portraying your favorite version of one of these classic tales. Make whatever props you'll need. Take this activity as far as you think your kids will enjoy. They can build backdrops, sew costumes, write their own script, and put on a play for family and friends. Some children are performers while others are not. Teach to your childs particular strengths and interests. Remember to make it about the fun, and the learning will take care if itself. Sewing and building are excellent skills to learn, they require measuring, cutting and accuracy, as well as patience.

TRY IT! Write your own version of the story, using bits and pieces of the ones you've read or something altogether different. Make sure that the key elements of the plot remain the same, but anything else can be changed.

CHECK IT OUT! As you stroll up Sunset Boulevard, you'll pass a store called Villains Vogue. Besides costumes and other souvenirs, this store carries a series of books labeled 'My Side of the Story'. We all know the Disney tales of heroines and victimized princesses, but is it really fair to only hear one side of a story? The Villains would say, NO, it's not. Each of these books has a double sided cover, with one side telling the familiar tale of Ariel (for example) and the other side tells the story from Ursula's point of view. Putting aside what you think you know about the tale, if you were to judge based on the two versions of events, who would you believe and why? Explain your answer below.

Liberty Square
Map

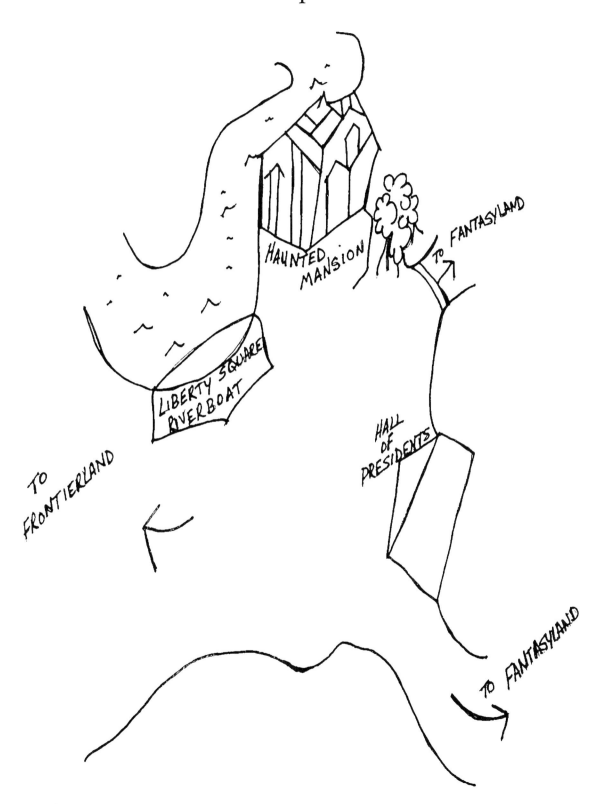

HAUNTED MANSION

TO FANTASYLAND

LIBERTY SQUARE RIVERBOAT

TO FRONTIERLAND

HALL OF PRESIDENTS

TO FANTASYLAND

Liberty Square

Vocabulary
Pilgrims
Mayflower
Harvest
Thanksgiving
Separatists
King James

If you are planning to study American history, you will want to spend at least a little time on how we came to be here; this country I mean. The Pilgrims came over on the Mayflower; a 65 day trip. The drinking water was stale, no water for bathing or washing, and only stale bread to eat. They landed on November 11, 1620. Many died from hunger and illness that winter. They prayed and asked God for help. In the spring, they befriended the natives and learned from them what foods would grow well, and gave them seeds to grow. That fall the harvest was so bountiful, they had a Feast of Thanksgiving. This was not the first or the last time they would do this.

The Separatists wanted to be separate from the church of England which was run by King James. They traveled to America for religious freedom; freedom to worship God the way they believed the Bible commanded which did not always agree with King James.

After the days of the Mayflower, and prior to the days of Liberty, lands an era of time called the Colonial days. A colony is a piece of land that is ruled over by another country, in the case of the first thirteen colonies of what would become the United States of America, that country was England. A great way to explore this time period is through career exploration.

Here are some of the jobs that were common during colonial times:

Cooper: They made barrels for storage, this was an occupation of necessity. Everyone needed these.

Silversmith: Like a jeweler, forming pretty pieces out of silver for the wealthy to adorn themselves.

Apothecary: Today we would call this person a pharmacist.

Blacksmith: They work with iron. Cast iron is black.

The Joiner is a woodsmith who makes fancy furniture, practical furniture pieces were made by a man from the wood he chopped down on his farm.

Cobbler: made shoes

Whitesmith: Someone who works with tin, so named because tin is white, as opposed to the blacksmith who worked with cast iron.

TRY IT! Make up an employment application for one of these positions.

What would the job require?

Write a resume for someone who would be looking for one of these jobs.

FIND OUT! Learn about the homes of the colonists. New Englanders had clapboard houses; Pennsylvania and New York had log cabins; Maryland had stone houses; Southern colonies had plantations (this could lead into a study of slavery in the United States, and the Civil War—Don't be afraid to follow your child's lead when it comes to studying history. The more you learn, the more you find it all fits together, and it doesn't need to be taught in any particular order.) Time lines are a good way to keep track of where in history an event is taking place. There are accordion style timelines available that you can fill in as you go.

 FIND OUT! What kind of foods did the colonists eat?

 TRY IT! Collect several recipes that were popular during colonial days, and make a few. Here is a website with a variety of recipes for you to sample:
http://www.1771.org/cd_recipes.htm

 TRY IT! Like a crock pot, put everything in a big pot in the morning and let it sit over the fire all day. Imagine having a fire going all day inside your house... in the winter it served double duty as a heat source, but in the summer? Whew! That must have been hot. No refrigeration available, and no boxed or canned goods.

 FIND OUT! The tree is older than the park. Which one was here first? Did they build the park around the tree, or did they build the park and then transplant the tree? See if you can find out.

☑ CHECK IT OUT! Locate a copy of the Declaration of Independence and find out exactly what those guys had in mind that day.

☑ CHECK IT OUT! The centerpiece of Liberty Square is called the Liberty Tree, where you'll find hanging thirteen lanterns. The Liberty Tree was a symbol for colonists before the revolutionary war, as a meeting place to discuss what they should do to protect their rights. Whenever there was trouble or something that needed to be discussed, a flag (usually red or white) would be flown from the top of a tree in the center of town and the Sons of Liberty would be alerted to gather at the tree. Because of these meetings, it soon became commonly referred to as the Liberty Tree. The thirteen lanterns hanging her represent the thirteen colonies.

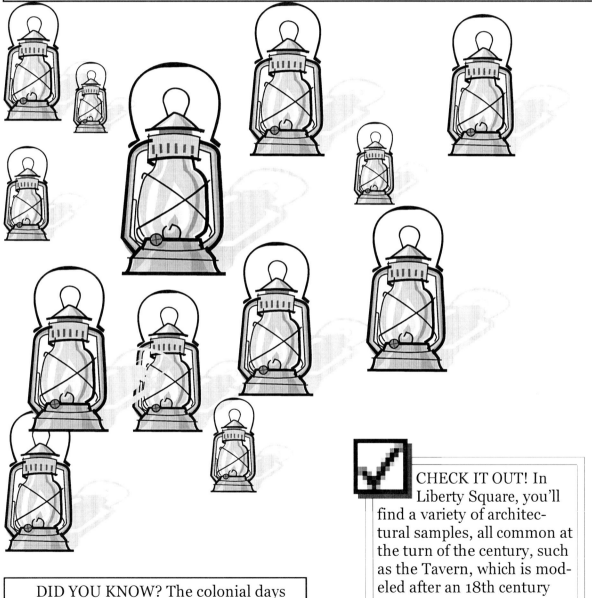

☑ CHECK IT OUT! In Liberty Square, you'll find a variety of architectural samples, all common at the turn of the century, such as the Tavern, which is modeled after an 18th century

? DID YOU KNOW? The colonial days ended in 1776 when the colonists declared their independence from England.

A fun and informative unit to study over the course of the year along with United States history is a unit on the historical significance and origination of our national holidays. Here's a few to get you started:

PRESIDENT'S DAY

VOCABULARY

Abraham Lincoln

George Washington

President Nixon

Revolutionary War

Civil War

Martyr

Inaugural Address

Gettysburg Address

Pioneer

Frontier

Edward Everett

David wills

Continental Congress

Declaration of Independence

The third Monday in February is commonly known as President's Day, honoring all past presidents. Abraham Lincoln was born on February 12th, 1809 and February 22nd is George Washington's birthday. They have more than that in common though. These two presidents are both famous for several reasons but primarily their fame comes from the battles that surround them. Washington's political career is surrounded by the history of the Revolutionary War, and Lincolns is surrounded by the history of the Civil War. It is hard to study US History and not have these two men appear as dominant figures.

FIND OUT! All that you can about these two presidents. What else did they have in common?

In 1971, president Nixon declared the third Monday of February as Presidents Day as opposed to the existing two holidays right in a row; one on February 12th and another on February 22nd. There is a practical reason for this. History saw the church honor martyrs annually, and due to a lot of persecution of Christians, the calendar was soon filled with a different Saint being honored each day. Eventually, November 1st was declared All Saints Day and all martyrs are honored at that time. Today, if there was a holiday for each president, we would have a holiday nearly every week just for that.

? DID YOU KNOW? Abe Lincoln was a homeschooled president. The Lincoln family worked a farm in Indiana. At the time, Indiana was like the wild frontier. Thomas Lincoln, Abe's father, was a pioneer. Abe was only sent to school for one year, after that all of his education came from his parents and was self taught. He earned his way to law school and eventually into the office of president.

Lincoln is well remembered for his ability to speak in public in front of large groups. He is remembered for many words. It is the quality that helped him to obtain the position of president.

CHECK IT OUT! Read Lincoln's First Inaugural Address. He pleads with his fellow country men to solve the disputes between the north and the south.

"Intelligence, patriotism, Christianity, and a firm reliance on Him, who has never forsaken this favored land, are still competent to adjust, in the best way, all our present difficulty."

His most famous speech is the Gettysburg Address given at the Soldiers National Cemetery in Gettysburg, Pennsylvania. The first days of July, 1863 left 7500 dead bodies on this ground, a number greater than the city's entire population. David Wills purchased land to bury and honor those fallen men. Edward Everett, a famous speaker was scheduled to M.C. the event. President Lincoln was included in the ceremony just a couple of weeks before it was to transpire. He was asked to simply to give a few closing remarks to officially dedicate the land. He finished writing his speech the night before the ceremony

Everett spoke for two hours, and yet his words are all but forgotten. It is the brief remarks of Lincoln that have been remembered throughout history. It is worth noting that in under three minutes, he did not neglect to mention the authority of God.

Many scholars have studied Lincoln's famed words.

CHECK IT OUT! Search for "analysis of the Gettysburg Address" and you will find numerous writings by various experts on these words, their careful crafting, and even opinions about underlying meanings.

 TRY IT! The Gettysburg address is only two minutes long, see if you can memorize it.

 SHARE IT! Perform this famous speech for others.

George Washington is most commonly known as the first President of the United States. While this is a true statement, it is not the complete story. The thirteen colonies had elected several presidents prior to the Revolutionary War, so Washington could not be the first ever president of this country. However, it was not until the Continental Congress authorized the Declaration of Independence that this nation would become a country, the United States. Washington was the first to be elected president of this new nation.

 CHECK IT OUT! At WWW. BARTLEBY.COM there is a copy of George Washington's first Inaugural Address. The formal English is not what we are accustomed to reading. This is an excellent assignment in both literature and history. The speech is eloquent and intelligent, and gives all credit to "...the Almighty Being..." "Great Author..." and His "...Invisible Hand...".

TRY IT! Play President Guess Who! This is a two player game, so for a large group, everyone can play with a partner. Post a list of all the U.S. Presidents, including photos if you are able, and various biographical information. Then, have each person write on a piece of paper (secretly) the name of one of the presidents. They should fold their paper in half and set it aside, remembering who they chose. Each person alternates with their partner asking yes or no questions to determine by process of elimination which president their partner wrote down. Each person must answer honestly, but can only answer yes or no. The first one to guess who their partner chose wins, this is a quick game (usually 10 minutes or less) and is a great way to pass the time. Players may use paper and pencil to keep track of questions they already asked and the answers to those.

FIND OUT! Earlier you searched for things that Lincoln and Washington had in common. Now, search for major differences. What did you find?

 CHECK IT OUT! See the Hall of Presidents for more fun and interesting trivia and activities

MEMORIAL DAY

The first Memorial Day was held on May 30. It was originally a tradition started by southern women to pay respect to the fallen soldiers of the Civil War. It gradually became a day to honor the men and women who had died in any war that the United States has been involved in.

Each year, individuals and groups around the country participate in events that honor our country's fallen soldiers. The third U.S. Infantry places and American flag at each and every one of the 260,000 graves at Arlington National Cemetery.

Taps is often heard at Memorial Day ceremonies. This 'lights out' bugle call was instituted by General Daniel Butterfield. It is used in the military to proclaim the end of the day and also at funerals to proclaim the end of a life. There are a few versions of the lyrics. This is the way I learned it when I was young.

Day is done,
gone the sun,
From the hills,
from the lake,
From the skies.
All is well,
safely rest,
God is nigh.

Thanks and praise,
For our days,
'Neath the sun,
Neath the stars,
'Neath the sky,
As we go,
This we know,
God is nigh.

 TRY IT! Interview a veteran. If you don't already know one, ask around in your church or contact the VA to see if they can help you locate someone who would be willing to tell their story. Www.va.gov/directory will provide you with a regional directory to help you find an office near you. Get permission and record the interview so that this soldier's story will never be forgotten.

FLAG DAY

On June 14th, 1777, Congress set up a committee to design a national flag to represent a unified country. This was after the Civil War had ended. It would not be a nationally honored item until one hundred years later on June 14th, 1877.

? DID YOU KNOW? Harry Truman would be the president to declare Flag Day on June 14th a holiday. Do you know when that was?

 CHECK IT OUT! On your drive to your vacation destination, you will likely pass a McDonald's. Their flags are flown in this order from top to bottom; USA flag, state flag, McDonald's flag. See if you can find an example of this.

? DD YOU KNOW? The American flag stands here above all the others. It should be flown daily at all public institutions, polling locations, and schools. When displayed on a flat surface, the blue field belongs in the left upper corner. Whenever a citizen is in the presence of the flag, they should stand with their right hand over their heart. Carriers of the flag must keep it from touching anything below it, especially the ground. When flown or carried beside another flag, such as state or organizational, the country flag must always be held above any other.

✋ TRY IT! Learn the Pledge of Allegiance to the United States Flag together as a family if you do not know it.
Learn the Pledge to the Christian flag also. Both are printed for you below.

I pledge allegiance to the flag of the United States of America, and to the Republic for which it stands. One nation under God, indivisible, with liberty and justice for all.

The Christian flag is white with a blue square in the upper left corner and a red cross within that square designed by Charles Overton in 1897.

I pledge allegiance to the Christian Flag and to the Savior for whose Kingdom it stands. One Savior, crucified, risen, and coming again with life and liberty to all who believe.

For each national holiday that you can find, answer these questions:

What year did this first become a holiday?

What were the events that caused this particular event to be celebrated?

What was going on in the country at the time?

Who was the President at the time?

What were his reasons for declaring this particular event cause for a national holiday?

Do people continue to celebrate/recognize the holiday in the same way that they did at first? If not, what are the differences?

A similarly themed unit and also lots of fun is the Patriotic Songs unit. How many can you think of? Here are some to get your study started:

"God Bless America"

Irving Berlin arrived in America in 1886, at the age of five. He joined the army during WWI and wrote, "God Bless America" as a marching song for the soldiers. On November 11, 1938, Kate Smith sang it on the radio and listeners loved it.

"America the Beautiful"

In 1893, Katherine Lee Bathes wrote a poem about the amazing sites she saw on a visit to Pike's Peak in Colorado. It was eventually matched with music from a hymn that went well with the words.

"America"

In 1831, Lowell Mason asked his friend Samuel Francis Smith to find a song in a German song book that the children of his church could sing. He found a tune he liked and wrote his own words to it. "America" was first sung at the Park Street Church in Boston, Massachusetts on July 4th. The music came from a hymn by Henry Carey.

"The Star-Spangled Banner"

In 1814 Francis Scott Key, from a British ship, watched the flag over Fort McHenry. As long as the flag remained, he knew the English had not prevailed. The original tune is by John Stafford Smith. That particular flag can be seen at Smithsonian Institute in Washington D.C. It is 32 feet long, 27 feet wide. It has 15 stars, 15 stripes, and 11 holes shot through it.

Yankee Doodle

This little diddy was written by Dr. Shackburg to play a joke on the colonists. It has many verses, can you find them all? Doodle is another word for foolish.

FYI — Liberty Square covers the time period in US history of the Colonial years through the years of the New Republic.
Hall of Presidents tells the story of the Constitution, established in 1789 (see the year on the front of the building?)

TRY IT! Editors of Weekly Reader Magazine present five basics of citizenship; honesty, compassion, respect, responsibility, and courage. Using a concordance and a topical index, create a devotional Bible study based on these characteristics. What doe God say about these traits, and how does that translate into the way we behave toward Him and toward others?

"Around our house we say JOY comes from putting Jesus first, Others second and Yourself last." J.O.Y.

```
F A N S N O I T U L O V E R F R S
R S I T N D J H M F O O D U L E S
O D O T O E K E E G K I C T A P S
N F R R Y T R A M Y F U S G G R Y
T G E G H I S T O R Y W D J E A J
I N V H C O N G R E S S E L T I F
E N E V I D L O I V D U G A T S E
R H C D T H A O A A Y L D R Y E A
R G X D I F C O L R R I G U S B C
E F Z D Z S M O G B D N R G B D I
I I N D E P E N D E N C E U U G R
T I R E N C Y R T N U O C A R E E
O O R E E N O I P Y Y L V N G H M
N O W A S H I N G T O N F I M S A
```

WORD SEARCH

History	Flag	Revolution	Country
Memorial	Taps	Martyr	Inaugural
Washington	Praise	Pioneer	Congress
Lincoln	Bravery	Frontier	Gettysburg
Independence	President	America	Citizen

Liberty Bell

I don't know about you, but I remember this story as they made this bell, rang it once and it cracked... sounds to me like poor workmanship rather than integral national history. But, then there is this museum where the bell is on display, which seems like it wouldn't be there if it didn't have some significance... So, I had to ask, what is the story with this bell?

It was originally cast in France to honor the 50th anniversary of William Penn's Charter of Privileges and the founding of Pennsylvania. Isaac Norris, speaker for the assembly and a Quaker chose the quote, "Proclaim liberty throughout the land unto all the inhabitants thereof" from Leviticus 25:10. The line immediately preceding this verse in the Bible is "And ye shall hallow the fiftieth year". Surrounding the replica bell in Liberty Square in the Magic Kingdom stand thirteen flags, one for each of the original colonies.

The bell did crack when it was first tried out, before it was even used. John Pass and John Stow were hired to melt it down and recast it, making it an American made product. The replica you see here is exact (minus the crack) because it was cast in the same mold as the original. The bell served our country well as it rang for the Continental Congress(1774), the signing of the Declaration of Independence (July 1776), and other important events in Philadelphia. It became known as the Bell of Revolution, and was hidden during the British Invasion, to protect it. After eighty years of continual use, it cracked again. In 1846, it was rung for the last time in honor of George Washington. It now holds its own place of honor in Philadelphia's Historic District. It can be seen in Independence Hall near the corner of Market and 6th street. (Ready to plan your next field trip?)

Other important events that earned a ringing of the bell:

September 3, 1783, rung for Treaty of Paris (end of war)

July 8, 1835 rung for the death of Chief Justice Marshall and cracked.

On July 8, 1776, it rang out loud and clear, Philadelphia Declaration of Independence was read for the first time.

 TRY IT! While you are in this area, step inside the Hall of Presidents, where you'll (hopefully) recognize some of our nations great leaders.

Hall of Presidents

The address on this building is 1787, the year that the Constitution was ratified. The paintings in the grand hall entry to this Philadelphia style colonial meeting house, include Jefferson, Eisenhower, Kennedy, Carter, Roosevelt, Lincoln and more. Once inside, you'll get a good look at all of the men who have served in this role from George Washington to George W. Bush.

 CHECK IT OUT! Pay close attention to the clothing worn by each president; does it show the changes in our culture, and the formal business suit?

What aspects have changed with the times and which have remained the same?

Disney has gone to great lengths to get the details just right for these animatronic figures. The costuming department studied not only the styles of dress for each man, but also the types of stitching and materials accurate for the time period.

 DID YOU KNOW? Abraham Lincoln was the first audio animatronic life size person. He was introduced to the world at the 1964-65 New York World's Fair.

The great leaders of our nation were men of prayer. Washington prayed before leading his men to battle the British...Lincoln... Ben Franklin, while never a president was a national leader and opened each meeting of the Continental Congress with words of prayer.

When you exit the Hall of Presidents theater, you will be in a gift ship. Don't be in a rush to get through these. There are many books available here that you may find valuable to your history unit. Also, you can look up your name and its history here. For a fee, you emay even be able to obtain a copy of your family crest. You can explore this area without spending any money and it is sure to add to your studies, maybe even inspiring interest in a new subject.

 DID YOU KNOW? You can find your family crest in the United Kingdom pavilion at Epcot also, or you can make your own. Check out Vacation Education Epcot for step by step instructions.

 CHECK IT OUT! Go to www.whitehouse.gov/history/presidents for biographical information on all presidents from George Washington to George W. Bush.

Liberty Belle Riverboat
Steamboat from Mark Twain era

The four story steamboats that were made famous through the books of Mark Twain (Samuel Clemens), brought forth a method of transport that was fast and inexpensive. They were poorly built, but grandly designed with wide staircases, luxurious quarters and lounges. They were a common gathering place for gamblers and their popularity is replicated by the riverboat casinos of modern day. It was only a few decades before the railroad put them out of use as a practical mode of transportation. A small number of cities like Cincinnati, Ohio have made an attempt to revitalize these beauties of the river, but your best chances of getting to ride one might be at Walt Disney World's Magic Kingdom.

The Liberty Belle shows off the grandeur of the steamboats that traversed our nations great rivers carrying passengers and products. It makes its run through the Rivers here around Tom Sawyer island, a playscape for all ages and an honor to the author, Mark Twain.

CHECK IT OUT! A great way to start your research of steamboats is a book written by Mark Twain titled, "Life on the Mississippi"

FIND OUT! Plot your path! You will need push pins and a large world map. Look up river boats and steamboats online or at the library. Every time you learn about another one of these water mansions, mark its location on the map with a pin. Cover it with contact paper and you can trace the boats path with a dry erase marker.

TRY IT! You can take a ride on the Liberty Belle, and possibly even have a chance to steer her, if you ask. You don't need a pilots license since the boat actually runs on an under water rail, but you might get a certificate to remember the experience. Samuel Clemens made his living driving these boats, and when he wrote about life on the river he used the name Mark Twain, words that to a ship captain mean safe water.

The Haunted Mansion

American history would not be complete without the legends of haunted houses to entertain us and frighten us just a little. Integral to the story of a haunted house is the presence of a haunt or haunts, namely ghosts or spirits of unrest, usually because of an untimely or particularly traumatic end to their life.

Disclaimer: We DO NOT believe in ghosts. We are very confident that the Bible clearly tells us the fate of the dead, and we don't think they are hanging out in people's houses, having dinner parties or inviting the living to join them, however, we present this unit for the FUN of it.

DID YOU KNOW? The Haunted Mansion opened in 1971. **?**

Vocabulary

Legend

Ghost

Tombstones

Hudson River Dutch Gothic

X. Atencio

Marc Davis

Claude Coats

Yale Gracey

Leota Toombs

Unlike stereotypical haunted houses, Walts design for the Haunted Mansion left the inside to the ghosts but kept the exterior meticulously maintained. But, even with this flaw, the theming begins before you enter the house. Check out the humorous side of the attractions creators in the tombstones which play on the names of some of the people involved in making the ride come to be. This building is designed along the lines of 19th century Hudson River Dutch Gothic architecture. It replicates the wealthy estates that would have sat along the Hudson River in New York City. The funny tombstones are word plays on the names of some of the Imagineers who worked on the attraction. Look for gags!

Now, as any good haunted house should, this one has its own story of origin. Ask any cast member standing outside the gates to tell you the story, it's in their training material. Here's the basic storyline as it was told to us by the cast member we stopped outside the mansion. Of course, every good story in WDW begins with a real person. Yale Gracey, leader of the special effects team is the inspiration for this story's title character. Leota Toombs (yes, that is her real name) is the costume designer.

DID YOU KNOW? X. Atencio wrote song "Grim grinning ghosts" **?**

A very wealthy family, the Gracey's, built Gracey Mansion on Indian burial ground even though previous owners had many 'unlucky' circumstances. Strange events took place from the first day they began to live there. You can read about these on the headstones as you approach the entrance. In the first scene of the house, the octagonal shaped room stretches to show pictures of the strange events surrounding the deaths of many of the Gracey family members. Eventually, Master William Gracey Jr. was the only surviving family member with no wife or children. One rainy night, a gypsy woman named Madame Leota knocked on the door. She was welcomed in and her powers must have won over the Master, because she was invited to stay on in the house. Master Gracey lived alone and so invited her to stay on as his companion. They became good friends, but Master Gracey longed for a young bride who could give him children to carry on his family name. Madame Leota became quite comfortable with the lifestyle provided here, and was jealous when Master Gracey announced that he would go out to find a wife who could bring him heirs. He left the mansion to travel the nations searching for this woman and returned with a young, beautiful fiance. Leota, in her jealousy lured the young bride to the attic the night before their wedding, presumably to try on her dress, only to lock her into an attic trunk. In the morning, Master Gracey was devastated when he could not find

his bride. He searched, but and so believing hung himself in pictures in the the lights go dark, to see Master there. Some claim searched and couldn't find her, she had left him, the attic. When the foyer stretch, and look up at the ceiling Gracey still hanging that they have.

By the time cated the body, she When it was time the hearse, there that's her you saw one of the staff lo- was already dead. to put the coffin into was no body. Maybe hanging from the

rafters in the foyer? Madame Leota scared away the horses that were supposed to pull the hearse, which is why it remains parked in front of the house; no one ever came back for it. They ran away so fast, their powerful hooves left marks deeply embedded in the pavement. Can you find them? To this day, no one has found the body of the bride. The wedding guests, realizing what Leota had done, were furious, and threw her into the river. In an attempt to cast some type of spell, instead of being drowned, she was instead shrunken to the size of a doll. When she was pulled out of the river, she put a curse on everyone, and everything, that nothing could move forward, but would always stay just as it was. The ballroom dancers are forever dancing, the bride is missing, Master Gracey hangs in the attic; but it backfired on her. She also is doomed to remain in her state. Look for her towards the end of the ride, her shrunken image greets you as you are leaving the mansion. She is asking you to stay on at the mansion. Master Gracey's will states that the service staff may keep and share all the property and riches, unless another is willing to stay on and be an adopted Gracey. The guests, I mean ghosts, will tell you there's ninety nine haunts; there's always room for one more. If you decide not to stay, watch out, some of them might try to follow you home.

One of the great things about Walt Disney World is that all of the cast members are happy. Everywhere you go, they are happy to see you and to help you. If you have noticed this, you may wonder why the cast members working in the Haunted Mansion are so darn rude. This is the one place in Disney parks where you'll find unfriendly cast members. This is because they are playing their part in the story. The staff all want you to feel unwelcome so you won't want to stay on and they can inherit the riches of the Gracey family.

Many different versions of this story have popped up. Here are some of what we found. In Disneyland Paris, the ride is called Phantom Manor, the phantom is in love with a woman about to be married to someone else. On the wedding night, he kills the groom and forces the bride to live with him forever. An alternate WDW story is that the bride is waiting for her groom, her friend tells her that he is really a pirate and she tosses her ring from an attic window, then jumps after it. He shows up to find her dead and hangs himself. Some say they can see an indentation of the brides ring in a brick in the walkway as guests are exiting.

 DID YOU KNOW? The ride cars are called Doom Buggies.

RUMOR HAS IT! We heard that the Haunted Mansion was originally intended to open in Disneyland as a walk through with maids and butlers leading the way and telling the story of a man who killed his young bride in an angry rage, she came back to haunt him, he was so disturbed, he hung himself. Many different versions of this tale have surfaced since then. See if you can find the real story.

Over the years, the Disney company has made a lot of changes and many of the original attractions are changing, or being replaced. This one has been a favorite for generations, so enjoy it while you can. We expect it to be around awhile since it just experienced a remodel in 2007, which by the way adds to the storyline. The scene with the "bride" is either Leota trying to attract a husband and when unsuccessful, killing her prey, or it fits in with the "unlucky" events that happened before Master Gracey took up residence.

 FIND OUT! Try to get a cast member to tell you the new story line (if there is one) to go along with the added scenes.

Frontierland Map

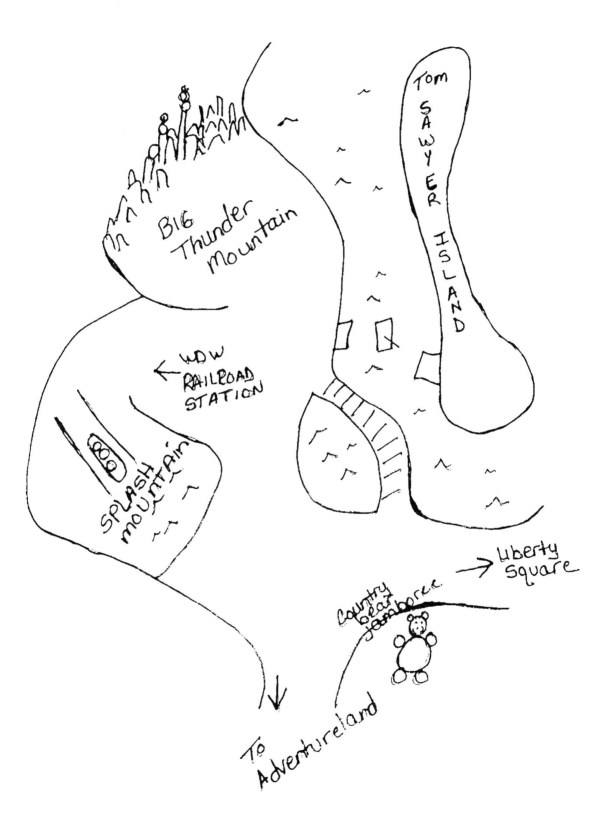

Frontierland

Vocabulary List

Cowboys

Cattle drives

Davy Crockett

Pecos Bill

Gold Rush

Daniel Boone

Stalagmites

Stalagtites

Transcontinental Railroad

Gold Rush

Louisiana Purchase

Thomas Jefferson

"Frontierland is a tribute to the faith, courage and ingenuity of the pioneers who blazed the trails across America." -Walt Disney.

Take a journey through the wild west in this land of cowboys and cattle drives. It is the land of Davy Crockett and the wooded frontier, Pecos Bill and the Gold Rush.

 TRY IT! A pioneer is someone who does something first and makes a way for others to follow. Be the first in your group to try out some of the big rides in this land.

DID YOU KNOW? Cowboy songs were not just a way for the boys to pass the time, but the slow steady melody helped to calm the cows and prevent a stampede. **?**

This area was part of the original plans for the Magic Kingdom, opening with it in 1971. At that time, there were only three attractions.

The Walt Disney World Railroad Station was one of the original attractions. It was torn out and rebuilt in 1982, and that is the structure that you see there today. The Country Bear Jamboree was part of Walt's design as well. The third attraction is no longer part of the Magic Kingdom. The Davy Crockett Explorer Canoes were real canoes that took guests on a ride down the Rivers of America. It was only part of the park for 12 years and then was closed.

✋ TRY IT! The Frontierland Trading Post has a rock collection. There is a table here where the kids can take some time to identify various rocks found while mining. They are all labeled and identified for you on the sides with a mixture of various stones in the center. It is just the right height for kids to stand at and search through the stones looking for the ones they want. You could have them try to find one of each kind. There are bags available to fill and for a fee you can take some home.

There are many famous pioneers. Daniel Boone is one who is known for his courage and ability to tame a wild frontier. He blazed a trail through the countryside and wilderness that generations after him would follow.

📖 FIND OUT! There is a roller coaster ride in Frontierland that takes you past a skeleton. To figure out which one it is, you will need to either ride every attraction until you see a skeleton, or study roller coasters and figure out how to determine which attractions in this park qualify.

📖 FIND OUT! How much do you know about Daniel Boone? He said, "The religion I have is to love and fear God, believe in Jesus Christ, do all the good to my neighbor, and myself that I can, do as little harm as I can help, and trust on God's mercy for the rest." -Daniel Boone. Read more about Daniel Boone and the frontier that he explored in A True, Brief History of Daniel Boone.

📖 FIND OUT! Two rides start out in caves where you can see stalagmites and stalagtites, which ones are they?

📣 SHARE IT! Daniel Boone and Davy Crockett are often confused; some people even think that they are one in the same. Find out as much as you can about each of them, and share what you've learned with others. Can you think of ways to help yourself and others to tell these two famous frontiersmen apart?

✅ CHECK IT OUT! Each building's 'address' number tells guests where in your timeline its architectural elements belong.

❓ DID YOU KNOW? During Boone's lifetime, particularly the 1770's to 1790's, the threat of Indian attack where Boone lived was so great that they didn't even hold worship services without having armed guards on duty. Imagine having soldiers outside your church every week.

 TRY IT! How good of an explorer are you? Try the game, "Oregon Trail" or something similar and find out if you can make it across the country alive.

Walt portrays the frontier in a way that glorifies westward expansion. His intention was to tell the stories the way a child would see it, the purpose always being to provide good family entertainment. He omits the history that pertains to people who did not benefit from the settlement of the west. There is always more than one way to tell a story.

CHECK IT OUT! When Liberty Square meets Frontierland, look at the pavement. Do you see the Mississippi river? There is a dark line of cement across the walkway. You are now crossing the Great River that divides the eastern frontier (represented in Liberty Square) and the western frontier (represented in Frontierland).

TRY IT! The Frontierland Shootin' Arcade, olde west style guns shoot at stuff to make it move or sound off. Try your hand at some target practice. Could you be a pioneer? Would you be able to shoot up some grub or would your shooting skills leave you hungry?

TRY IT! Woody's Cowboy Camp. It might be helpful to have seen the Toy Story movies if you want your kids to recognize the characters, but it is not necessary for the enjoyment of the show. It's a very interactive show, all the kids in the audience are invited to join Woody and friends as they sing cowboy songs and play games. Check your daily program guide for scheduled show times.

The Diamond Horseshoe Saloon once held a restaurant and stage where regular shows were held.

"We still have a badge our daughter received for being a star when she was called on stage to be part of the show. That was a real magical moment."

This location is now a meet and greet for Toy Story characters. We hope that Disney execs will see that Walt's original idea of creating a place for families to have fun together still has great merit. Perhaps even more so today as families are segregated by age and gender and for many the family vacation is the only extended time they spend together as one.

CHECK IT OUT! The Tall Tale Inn and Café. It's proprietor is Pecos Bill. Look on the wall for the story of this restaurant's beginnings.

See if you can find
BILL'S CODE OF THE WEST

Song of the South
Splash Mountain

Vocabulary List

Uncle Remus

Joel Chandler Harris

James Baskett

This attraction is based on the 1946 Disney film "Song of the South", with memorable characters like Brer Rabbit, born and bred in a briar patch, sly Brer Fox, and dimwitted Brer Bear. The character of Uncle Remus, the storyteller, was created by newspaper cartoonist, Joel Chandler Harris, and is likely based on a number of old storytellers that Harris had met during his life. This musical production is a reenactment of stories that Harris had heard passed down for many years.

The Uncle Remus stories created by Harris were some of Walt Disney's favorites as a child. He chose this film as the first Disney production to use a combination of live action with animation, to capture not just the stories themselves, but also the characterization of the storyteller.

The ride cars are hollowed out logs that seat up to eight passengers.

"There is a surprise drop. I say surprise because although I know it's coming, there are several small drops that I always think are the big one, but aren't and then I get busy paying attention to the things going on in the ride story that I forget to count how many teasers there are that I am always surprised by the big drop at the end."

For the technical riders, it is 52 1/2 feet long, at a 45 degree angle, traveling at 40mph.

"There is a nice play area underneath this ride called "The Happy Place" that is perfect for the baby swappers."

✓ CHECK IT OUT! As you exit Splash Mountain, you will find the Briar Patch Gift Shop. If B'rer Fox and B'rer Bear really want to find B'rer Rabbit, they should stop by here since this is obviously his home. Look up at the ceiling (this is where you'll find some of the best things in WDW), you'll see where Rabbit has set up a homestead amongst the briars.

TRY IT! Have each person in your group count the number of one of these items that you see: frogs, turtles, or carrots. When you get off the ride, compare to see if your numbers agree.

❓ DID YOU KNOW? James Baskett, the actor who plays the part of Uncle Remus, also did the voices of the butterfly, Brer Fox, and Brer Rabbit.

Big Thunder Mountain Railroad
Must Be 40 Inches Tall to Ride

Vocabulary List
Gold Rush
Roller Coaster
LaMarcus Adna Thompson
Potential energy
Kinetic energy
Kinematics
Friction
Sam Brannan
James Marshall
John Sutter
Prospector
surveyors

Like everything else in WDW, this attraction has a storyline. Try to imagine it; you are boarding a mining car left behind after the gold rush; and traveling a path carved out of the mountain by long gone miners. Can you identify all the real tools left behind by the miners who left with or without their fortunes?

✓ CHECK IT OUT! Study the Gold Rush. Visit www.pbs.org for an excellent premade unit study on the California Gold Rush with discussion questions and activities for 4th Grade on up in the subjects of history, economics, geography and civics. Many thought provoking questions are posed in this study, and can be easily steered toward a Biblical Worldview, such as, "What are the positive and negative aspects of unbridled capitalism? The consequences?

Another great resource for Gold Rush unit study ideas can be found at
Www.easyfunschool.com/article1075.html
This site lists many additional useful sites as well.

❓ DID YOU KNOW? Thunder Mountain is the tallest mountain in all of Florida at 197 feet.

TRY IT! Write It! You are a citizen of Sacramento, CA in 1848. Write three diary entries, one before the gold rush, one during and one after it's over.

✋ *Great Group Activity!*

TRY IT! Hold a Gold Rush Party. Make invitations that look like a news article announcing all the gold that has been found. List your address as the location of the find, and state the time that your camp store will open to sell supplies to the prospective miners. Instruct everyone to dress appropriately, and bring a shovel.

Pan For Gold:
Supply List:
**one disposable pie plate per person (use a hammer and nails to poke small holes in the bottom)
 **a large plastic tub to fill with dirt, water and gold
**assorted beans, from split peas to kidney beans
**one can of gold spray paint
** newspaper
** bags for miners to take home their findings

　　　Use the directions below to make the gold. Fill the tub with water and dirt and mix in some gold pieces. For the activity, each miner will place their pan in the water and scoop up some dirt and sift through it to find gold. Do a little research so you can show them how it's done.

Making the Gold:
Lay out the beans on newspaper (better to do this outside if possible), and spray paint them gold; when dry, flip them over and spray the opposite side. You will use these to pan for gold and also for scavenging for gold. How much you need depends on the number of guests you will have. One bag of beans per two to three guests, and one can of spray paint will cover about four to five bags of beans. Do this activity with caution if you have children in your group who might try to eat them, paints can be toxic.

Scavenging For Gold:
Hide the gold pieces of various sizes, kidney beans are big nuggets and split peas are gold dust. If you have a wooded area or a trail, hide the pieces along the trail.

"For the smallest children, we put the pieces on the ground in plain sight in a garden area and gave them boundaries in which to look. For the older children, we made maps and gave them compasses so that they were also learning orienteering as they searched for gold."

Getting Paid:

The rush for gold was the alluring promise of great wealth; a life with no financial worries. Set up a surveyors office. You will need some prizes and a kitchen scale.

"We made recipes that would have been common in 1849 California and posted a menu board. As the prospectors came in the surveyors office, we weighed their gold and they could purchase their lunch items based on the weight of their gold."

"We traded the kids pennies equal to the weight of the gold they collected. The kids really felt rich."

More Fun Stuff:

*Take photos of the prospectors in their mining clothes and use photo editing software to make black and white pictures that look antique.

*Make root beer together.

*Make beef jerky together.

*Set up a mining camp outside with tents or large branches and a tarp.

*Cook up some grub over an open fire; readily available foods at the time would include potatoes, and wild meats.

*Make a solar box oven (most Scouting manuals have directions).

FIND OUT! It's 1849, and you are planning to head out to California to seek your fortune, but there are several travel options that will get you there. Using a map, plan out the route that you would choose from where you live. Make a list of the supplies that you would need to take with you?

TRY IT & FIND OUT MORE! Let's assume that you have chosen a land route. How many steps does it take to get to California? Before you do this activity, make a guess and then when you are done, compare and see how close your guess was to the actual answer.

Step One: Look up and find out how many miles are there between your town and San Francisco (this can be done on Mapquest or AAA websites) .

Step Two: Measure your stride; take a normal step and have someone measure the distance from the back of one heel to the back of the other.

Step Three: Divide your answer from step two (in inches) into 63, 360 (the number of inches it takes to equal one mile). Now you know how many steps you have to take in order to walk one mile.

Step four: Multiply the answer from step three by the number of total miles you will be traveling (your answer from step one), and you will know how many steps it would take to get to the gold.

Are you ready to start walking?

You can continue on this same line of thinking by asking

*How many miles can I walk in one hour?

*How many hours a day could I reasonably walk?

*How many days would it take me to reach my destination?

✋ TRY IT! Go on a family treasure hunt. Start with a treasure map and clues. Here's how one family did it: (pirates went after jewels and gold coins, but your family can search for real treasure)

"We posted this sign on our daughter's bedroom door so she would see it as soon as she woke up.

Good morning birthday girl

We have something special for you!

There's a hidden treasure to find

Here's your first clue.

Start your day by looking for something new.

On top of her dresser, we put a new Young Women of Faith Bible, and the next clue. We continued leading her through the house, giving her small gifts including Scripture verses, and ending at a package we'd hidden in the basement."

Think you're not creative enough to come up with interesting clues? Try this idea:

"Have the kids make treasure maps and clues for you. If you can find the treasure, they get an A."

This is an activity that builds creative logic skills, and is a great, fun way to learn to follow sequenced instructions by practicing writing them in the correct order.

✋ TRY IT! Make a treasure map. Print or draw a map onto a piece of typing paper. Crumple the paper, then dab it with a wet tea bag to give it an aged look. Roll it up and tie it with raffia. Put it in a glass bottle with some sand and shells. You can hide the map and make clues to find it.

Country Bear Jamboree

The Grizzly Hall theater features an eighteen minute show starring country music sweetheart, Teddi Barra and country western singing group, Five Bear Rugs. They are joined by Melvin the Moose, Buff the Buffalo, and Max the deer, three wise cracking trophies mounted on the wall.

In comparison to many of the attractions that feature audio animatronics, this show has the added challenge of being up close and in person...er...bear and needs to be 'real' to the audience for an extended time. Attractions using this technology where guests ride past in a moving vehicle do not have the same necessity as the visual time frame is shorter.

CHECK IT OUT! A real country jamboree might be going on in your area. See if you can find one. Any kind of music festival will do.

We like the Country Bear Jamboree, but did not appreciate the movie based on the attraction. I personally have an aversion to stories with talking animals and humans co-existing... it just doesn't sit right with me.

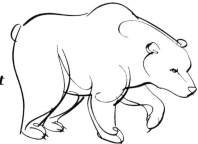

DID YOU KNOW? This attraction has some unique elements. It is an attraction that inspired a movie, not the other way around. The attraction was an original idea of Walt Disney and Marc Davis; plans were being made for it right before Disney died. The movie didn't come about until 2002.
Many of the Disneyland attractions were brought over to WDW, but in the case of this attraction, it was built first in Florida, and later added to Disneyland because it was so popular. It is still going strong at the Florida park, but was in California, it was replaced in 2001 by The Many Adventures of Winnie the Pooh.

TRY IT! Hold your own Country Jamboree. Make up some musical instruments, and put on a performance for your friends.

HERE ARE SOME IDEAS FOR
MUSICAL INSTRUMENTS
YOU CAN MAKE!

BANJO!
You will need:
Kleenex box
Rubber bands (large)
Optional:
Pencil
Paper towel tube

Step one: Decorate the Box.
Step Two: When dry, wrap rubber bands around the box lengthwise so they cross the hole in the middle.
Step Three: Optional, with a parents help, trace the round end of the paper towel tube onto the end of the box, and cut it out.
Step Four: Decorate and then place tube into hole in box. This is now your handle.
Step Five: Optional, slide the pencil under the rubber bands on top of the box on the end opposite the handle. This allows for better sound, but is not required.

TAMBOURINE!
You will need:
Two disposable tin pie plates
Plastic buttons
Masking tape
Large sewing needle and Thread

Step One: Attach the pie tins top to top, and tape them together, wrapping the masking tape around the edge.
Step Two: Decorate if desired, permanent markers work well. Nail polish is also a good permanent option (with plenty of adult supervision, of course).
Step Three: Sew the buttons onto the edge of the tins, leaving enough string for each one to reach the center of the tins.
**This will require a parents help. The needle will go through the tin, but does require pressure. So, use caution.
Step Four: Sew these all the way around. Go through the masking tape also, and this will automatically cover any sharp edges from the tin and protect little fingers.
Step Five: Shake!

CHECK IT OUT!

For older children and more complex designs for real working instruments, visit http://home.earthlink.net/~jbertles/

This is the site for a program called Bash the Trash. If you Google "Bash the Trash" it will come up also. It provides step by step instructions for using things you would normally throw away to create real working musical instruments.

GREAT IDEA FOR SCIENCE!

SHARE IT! Hold your own movie premier. Make invitations, prepare fancy food and drinks for the honored guests, and invite your closest friends to see your movie. Show your favorite Disney movie.

 TRY IT! A press release is issued in order to create interest in the upcoming film. Write a press release for your film you made or for an event or activity going on in your school or community. Take your written material and try to get your local newspaper to publish it.

Working the Magic

There are many jobs at the Magic Kingdom. The Disney cast members that you see are trained to take care of guests, but there are many more that you never see. The Utilidor tunnel system provides for an entire city of workers to go about making Magic for guests without ever being noticed. As homeschoolers, we have a unique opportunity to guide our children toward their God-given talents. Taking the time to explore careers allows you and your child to see where those talents and interests lie. Career exploration provides education that focuses on preparation for adult life, not just arbitrary knowledge.

Here is a sampling of the important jobs you might not see; each one of these is an opportunity to explore a possible future career. For a more comprehensive list, see "The Imagineering Field Guide to the Magic Kingdom". An Imagineer, if you don't already know, is Walt's word for an Imaginative Engineer– does that sound like you?

Concept Designer: do you have an idea for a new attraction? Would you like to see your imagination brought to life? This could be the job for you.

Landscape Architect: Do you love working on your garden, beautifying the plant life in your vicinity? Then, this might be the job for you... the biggest garden you've ever loved.

If you're a future thinker, and I mean even beyond Tomorrow Land and Future World kind of thinking, you could go to work as one of Disney's Master Planners, and help plan the attractions to come, maybe even the next park.

Designers: There are designers for props, graphics, costumes, lighting, sound effects and more. Putting together a day at Disney is like putting on a huge theater production.

Can you put a story together? Can you come up with creative names and slogans for the attractions? You could be a Disney writer.

 CHECK IT OUT! The Haunted Mansion's tombstones are the creative work of Disney writers.

The Project Manager is in charge of keeping everything organized and making sure things get done on time and up to Disney standards. The Construction Manager handles all the building issues and make sure everything is up to code. Do you have the attention to detail that this job requires?

If you went to Epcot and never left the Innoventions buildings, you might want to apply for a job with the research and development department. R&D gets to try out all the latest in technological advances to see how they can best be implemented into Disney magic.

Tom Sawyer Island

This is a great place to let the kids run off some steam. There is only one way off the island, so you can relax while they run around. Beware that while they can't just wander off the island without you, there are plenty of places to get lost, intentionally or otherwise. Explore the caves and secret passageways, escape routes and more. Bathrooms and water fountains are available on site. You'll have to cross the mighty Mississippi to get here, but you're in luck, rafts have been provided.

DID YOU KNOW? Fort Langhorne is from the Disney movie "Tom and Huck". Harper's Mill named after Harper Goff.

CHECK IT OUT! From the library and read Tom Sawyer or biography of Mark Twain. Good News Moms and Dads! According to the authors of the Core Knowledge series, Tom Sawyer is recommended reading for the upper elementary set. Samuel Clemens is the real name of the author of this book. Mark Twain is the pen name he used; it means safe water. Twain (Clemens) is from Hannibal, Missouri, just 90 miles east of Marceline where Walt spent much of his youth.

TRY IT! Visit Tom Sawyer island, ride the steam boat.

SHARE IT! Write a story using these vocabulary words:

feather stroke
Rudder
Starboard
Port
Bow
Stern
Fore
Aft
cast off
take up slack
simper paratus
'get out of irons'.

FIND OUT! Where the paintbrush is. Everyday a cast member hides a paintbrush on the island (it's one that Tom or one of his friends left out after whitewashing the fence). If you can find it, turn it into the captain of the raft as you head back to the Mainland. You will get a special prize.

USE THIS SPACE TO WRITE A BOOK REPORT ON TOM SAWYER
OR ANY MARK TWAIN/SAMUEL CLEMENS
WORK THAT YOU HAVE READ.

TITLE:_____

PUBLISHER:_____

YEAR OF COPYRIGHT:_____

MAIN IDEA:_____

_____

_____

_____

_____

PLOT SUMMARY:_____

_____

_____

_____

_____

_____

MY FAVORITE PART:_____

_____

_____

_____

USE EXTRA PAPER IF NEEDED.

Frontierland Train Station

This place is pretty tame compared to the Big Thunder Mountain Railroad, so tame that there are no height restrictions, All Aboard!

The WDW RR travels a clockwise route around the Magic Kingdom. If you board here at Frontierland; you can get off at Toon Town Square, or stay on board until the train arrives at Main Street USA. The train runs a continuous loop, and guests board and depart at each station. You can stay on for as long as you like. It is often a quiet place to take a break and enjoy the cool breeze and pleasant scenery if you, or your kids, or your feet need a short rest.

TRY IT! Disney offers several touring plans for guests who want to see more than the norm. "Behind the Magic of our Steam Trains" is a three hour tour that allows you to enter the park prior to opening. Park admission is required in addition to the cost of the tour ($40) . This tour is not recommended for children under ten.

 CHECK IT OUT! Look for a wooden leg name Smith. If you don't get this joke, then you need to rent Mary Poppins and have a

 DID YOU KNOW? At first these engines burned wood for fuel, now they burn oil.

The WDW RR team of trains is made up of four engines; The Lilly Belle (named after Walt's wife—this is also the name of the train Walt built in his backyard), Roy O. Disney (named after Walt's brother), Walter E. Disney (named after... do I really have to tell you who this one is named after?), and the Roger E. Braggie (named after a friend of Walt's, an imaginer who shared his passion for trains).

These real steam engines were originally built at Baldwin Locomotive Works of Philadephia, Pennsylvania. They were used for many years to haul passengers and freight in Mexico. They were purchased from Yucatan United Railways and refurbished for use by Disney in the 1960's.

FIND OUT! Walt had a great love for trains beginning in his boyhood days as a sales boy for Santa Fe RR. Thomas Edison had a similar job. Was this common for young boys, like a paper route today?

TRY IT! Set up a train set. Be sure that all connections meet and that the trains can not leave the track anywhere that you don't want them to. If you don't have a train set to build, there are often tables set up at ToysRUs stores, libraries or other places that are designated for children.

Would it be too obvious to suggest studying the history of trains and railroads?

Adventure Land
Map

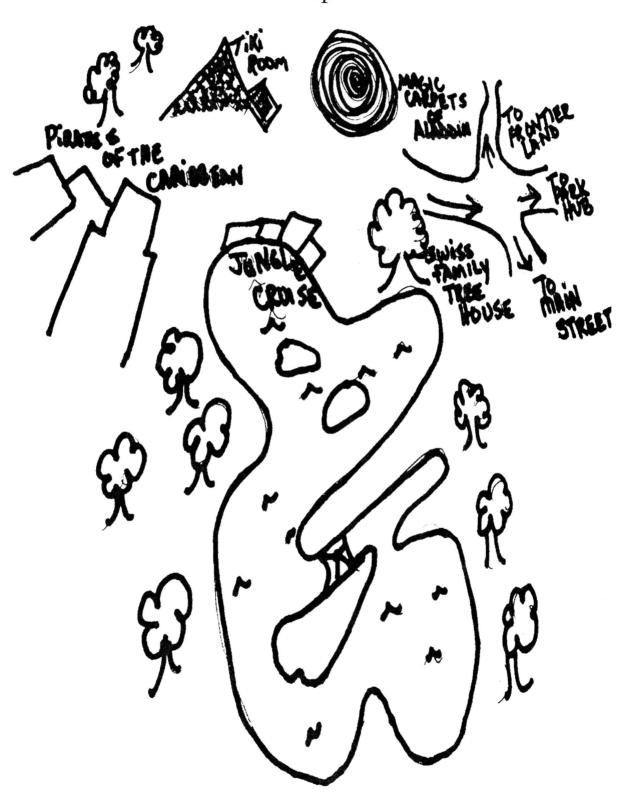

Adventureland

This is the place for world travelers and explorers. Once man figured out that he could venture out and not fall off the edge of the earth, he became quite adventurous. This area is a tribute to those explorers and all the adventures they've had.

The transition between Frontierland and Adventureland contains elements used to keep you from seeing anything from the other lands that would make the theming less believable. Adventureland showcases architecture from the Spanish islands, and Frontierland showcases architecture from the Southwestern United States, both very similar in style, creating a smooth flow from one area to the next.

CHECK IT OUT! See if you can find some of the old episodes from "True Life Adventures" series of documentary films. This was an old Disneyland television show. Whenever Walt introduced a new ride to the park, he would introduce the real life adventurer (like Davy Crockett) to the public through his show. You may be able to find several episodes on VHS at your video store or library. Our favorite is Johnny Appleseed.

Christopher Columbus

Pirates of the Caribbean

Vocabulary

Pirate

Christopher Columbus

Mark Davis

X. Atencio

Black Beard

Cargo ship

Merchant ship

Mutiny

Jolly Roger

Privateer

Vikings

Buccaneers

Compass

Telescope

This is one of Walt's originals, and although it has been redone in an effort to please the politically correct, it remains essentially the same in story. A pirate is a robber on the seas. After Christopher Columbus landed here, news of riches in silver and gold spread all across Europe. When the Spanish, who had laid claim to the land, tried to haul the treasures back to their homeland, the boats loaded with gems were too tempting for the pirates to resist.

"This was one of the first attractions to exit into a gift shop, many of the other attractions have followed suit. It's an excellent marketing strategy. You just rode the Pirates of the Caribbean, it was so cool, how can you possibly pass up a pirates cap and sword or a box of treasure for yer young'n?"

It takes a lot of talented Imagineers to make the story magic, but for this attraction, Marc Davis was an integral player in the sight gags that guests love to see over and over again. Davis is also famous for creating Tinker Bell and others. You will find his name honored here. Elements of the entrance to this attraction inspired by 400 year old Castillo de San Felipe del Morro in San Juan, Puerto Rico, a Spanish fort used to fight pirates. X. Atencio wrote "YoHo, YoHo (A Pirate's Life For Me).

> DID YOU KNOW? The attraction here at WDW is a copy (although not an exact copy as Walt did not like to repeat himself). The attraction first appeared at Disneyland, and was popular enough to be included in the plans for WDW.

TRY IT! Post a pirate's Code of Conduct to help remind your children of good character traits, like these:

TELL NO TALES (LIES)

SHARE YOUR TREASURE

KEEP THE SHIP NEAT

Pirate ships carried many more men than cargo ships and were able to quickly outnumber and overpower the crews of merchant ships. When people started to settle the new found land, the ships not only carried treasures (like gold and jewels), but also necessities such as food and supplies for the crew of the ship. The pirates never needed to go to a port to get supplies because they stole them from other ships. This made them difficult to apprehend.

The government of Spain and those of other countries eventually had to send military forces out to sea to fight the pirates. Some of these famous thieves were killed in battles, while others were arrested and imprisoned. Some were sentenced to death and publicly executed to set an example for anyone thinking of entering the vocation.

CHECK IT OUT! One of the most famous of all pirates in North America was Black Beard. His flag ship, Queen Anne's Revenge is now part of an archaeological site off the coast of North Carolina. You can learn more about the history of piracy along American borders and more about the dig itself through East Carolina University's Archaeological Conservation laboratory. Search for them online.

As you exit this ride, you will once again be in a gift shop. This was actually the first attraction to be designed in this way, but most of the others have since followed suit. Among the many pirate costumes and weaponry, you'll also find this a good source of books on the subject.

"Our experience has been that when it comes to books, Disney prices are equal to the suggested retail price, which may not be the best deal, but it is what you would pay in a high-end book market."

Some of the books we found interesting were 'The Buccaneers' by Iain Laurence and "A Pirate Research Guide' from the Magic Tree House series. The Magic Tree House set consists of one fiction story book for the kids to read (this is a series of historical fiction—a group of children travel into the past through their tree house), and a study guide to learn the "True Facts" about pirates.

There have been pirates all throughout history. For as long as there have been boats to sail out to sea, there have been thieves and robbers using them in their trade. This particular attraction personifies the pirate tales of what is consider the Golden Age of pirating. Around the 1600's and 1700's, there was much exploration going on around the world, with the new Americas being recently discovered. Merchants, explorers and anyone looking for a new life and opportunity ventured into the new land to see what could be found. They all traveled by ship, and became vulnerable to the attacks of sea robbers.

GREAT GROUP ACTIVITIES!

TRY IT! The Loyalty Line Up. While the pirates never followed the laws of any land, there were strict codes on board the ship. Anyone who broke these codes was considered a mutineer and receive a severe punishment. The mutineer causes a mutiny and the entire crew follows him. The object of the game is for the captain to uncover the mutineer to end the mutiny or for the mutineer to overthrow the captain and declare himself the new captain.

Here's How To Play:

Step 1: Select a Captain and send him out of the room .

Step 2: Secretly, amongst the group, someone volunteers to be the mutineer.

Step 3: The Captain is called back into the room.

Step 4: The mutineer must perform actions (this works best if everyone is in a circle), such as clapping their hands, tapping their foot, rubbing their head, etc. Whatever the mutineer does, everyone else must follow, trying not to let the Captain know who the mutineer is.

The Captain gets three guesses (less if you have a small group). If the Captain guesses correctly, the mutiny has been averted and the Captain maintains his position. If he fails to guess correctly, the mutineer reveals himself and claims himself the new Captain. Either way, the round is over and you begin again at Step 1.

TRY IT! Find The Traitor (Trader) This is a variation on the above game, designed on a similar premise. You will need a bandana for each player (it works best if the bandanas are not all the same. This game is a great memory activity.

How to Play:

Step 1: Each player ties a bandana around their wrist.

Step 2: Choose one person to be the captain.

Step 3: The captain stands inside the circle for thirty seconds trying to memorize what each of his crew looks like. Then, he leaves the room.

Step 4: Two of the crew members "trade" bandanas. They are the "traitors".

Step 5: The captain is called back in and stands in the middle of the circle again. He is given a set amount of guesses (usually three unless you have a small group, then only one or two). He must guess two people at a time and get both of them right to end the mutiny. If he guesses correctly, then he stays captain and play begins again. If he does not guess correctly, then the traitors reveal themselves and a new captain is chosen.

Pirates probably didn't really bury their treasure, they spent it as fast as they made it. Often a ship would be attacked only to find it carrying little more than food and standard supplies. But, there were tales of Spanish ships filled with gold discovered in the new land. Today, there are tales of pirate treasure buried somewhere in the Caribbean Islands. Both are more fiction than fact. But, classics like Treasure Island by Robert Louis Stevenson make for fun reading, allowing the imagination to explore the idea of finding a great buried treasure.

 TRY IT! Take your family on a search for real treasure! Visit these websites to learn how.

Letterboxing.org
"This is one of our favorite family activities. And it is practically free. We carry a small box with a notebook, pen and stamp in the car, so that wherever we travel, if we can get online, and there is one in the area, we try to find it."

Geocaching.com
"This activity is more expensive since you have to have a GPS unit to find the items, but there is more adventure and surprise in the items that others have left behind."

☑ CHECK IT OUT! The Vikings were pirates. In our study of Norway, we discuss King Olaf's receipt of the Gospel message. Olaf was a famous Viking, and on a raid in England, he learned of his Savior. He returned to his homeland to share this knowledge, declared the Bible the law of the land, and soon ended the Viking era. What happens next? Check out Vacation Education destination Epcot's chapter on Norway to find out more.

☑ CHECK IT OUT! From your local video store. The Pirates of the Caribbean movies. Knowing what pirates were like can cause us to apply one of two theories, either they were all about adventure and the high seas or they were all about murdering and pillaging on the high seas. But, it can sometimes be difficult to imagine them as just average guys trying to make their way through life, and being faced with decisions just like you and I and having to figure things out. We all make bad choices some times.
"I love when the two guys are the rowboat and the one guy holds up the Bible and says we have to start thinking about our immortal souls."

"My favorite scene, although gruesome, is when they one pirate has to choose death or a century of servitude on Davy Jones ship [Davy Jones was a famous pirate who sank enemy ships, so anytime anything went overboard, it was said to be sent to "Davy Jones Locker"]. The guy holds up his cross and says I'll take my chances. Then, he is martyred. I just think that is a great scene"

This movie should be considered carefully before watching with young children, but I think these scenes remind us of what Ephesians 2:8-9 really means for us.

Jungle Cruise

Vocabulary

Amazon

Mekong River

Asia

Congo

Nile

Bill Evans

Wathel Rogers

"The African Queen"

The jungle cruise begins in a misty rainforest in the Amazon, Mekong River in the wilds of uncharted Asia. Walt wanted to use real animals but realizing they are asleep much of the afternoon (the busiest time for the park), and their behaviors are quite unpredictable, he decided to use audio animatronics.

The attraction incorporates elements from the Amazon, Congo, Nile and Mekong rivers; plants and animals from all four, many of which wouldn't even be found on the same continent normally, let alone all on the same river. Study up on these real habitats and see if you can tell which animals don't belong, identify the 'errors' or variations from reality.

The Jungle Cruise is one of the attractions not based on a Disney film. Walt's original plan was to have real animals, but they were not predictable enough, and could not be trained to do the gags that these do. Look in the queuing area of this ride for tributes to people who worked here, like Bill Evans (hint: he was the landscape architect). And Wathel Roger's, jot down some of the other names you see and look them up when you get home. Were you able to guess what part they played in the creation and development of this area based on the clues given around their name?

? DID YOU KNOW? The idea for this attraction grew from a True Life Adventure episode in 1955 about a family of lions.

☑ CHECK IT OUT! The boats here were originally modeled after the ship "The African Queen".

To learn more about real animals, add one of the following local parks to your itinerary. Animal Kingdom, Sea World, Busch Gardens.

Swiss Family Robinson
Attraction: Swiss Family Treehouse

Vocabulary

Johann Wyss

Robinson Crusoe

Social mores

Cultural norms

This is a replica of the treehouse from the Disney movie based on the book by Swiss pastor Johann Wyss. It was the story of Robinson Crusoe that inspired Wyss to write the story in 1812. He intended it to be a teaching tool for his four sons. Most of the chapters in the book focus on Christian morals, and family values.

In 1960, Disney produced a film by the same name based on Wyss' novel. Some of Wyss' Christian elements were kept in Disney's film version. The characters are all members of a traditional Christian family. A kind, loving husband and father who puts his family above all else, and maintains a strong leadership role in his home, even when they have no home. A respectful, submissive wife who protects her children, honors her husband and puts God first. Siblings who look out for each other and while they don't always agree, they are still the best of friends.

The children are always obedient. Even when they were in the heat of argument and the two older boys are fighting, the sound of their father's voice stops them in their tracks. They are well trained. Even young Francis is obedient, although we can see that sometimes his heart is not in it.

What family wouldn't want to follow their example? They are a family working, living and playing together through bad times and good fortunes. They know how to receive real JOY—Jesus first, Others second, Yourself last.

When the boys find the pirates and their captives, they automatically think of saving them, even though it means risking their own lives. They have been trained to put others first.

They use ingenuity and improvisation to get what they need.

TRY IT! The next time you think you need to go to the store for something, pretend you've been shipwrecked on an island and you have to make do with what is on your ship (house). How long can you last with the supplies you already have?

? DID YOU KNOW? The family name is not Robinson. The name in the title comes from Robinson Crusoe, who inspired the story.

✔ CHECK IT OUT! From your local library. Start with Robinson Crusoe, then The Swiss Family Robinson. After reading these, watch the Disney version of the film; what similarities and differences do you notice between the book and the movie?

Can you pick out the elements of Robinson Crusoe that Wyss thought were worth using in his book?

FIND OUT! What social mores, and cultural influences were at play in the boys lives?

Examine the vast difference between how they treat Bertie when they think she is a boy in contrast to the way they treat her once they realize that she is a girl.

My two favorite quotes from the movie:

"For some boys school is a punishment, for others a reward." Ernst

"If only people could have all this and be satisfied?" Father

Tiki Room

Vocabulary

Tiki

Maori

Mythology

folklore

Genesis

creation

DID YOU KNOW? That there isn't really such a thing as a Tiki bird? Here's what our research uncovered; be sure to use this information to uncover even more on your own.

Occassionally, we hear objections to anything Disney on the grounds that it is anti-God. On the whole I disagree, but this is one attraction where I would have to agree and so place a warning to Christian parents that there are elements of idol worship and references to angry gods. Rather than avoid the parks altogether, read on to see how we handled these elements in our family.

In Maori mythology, Tiki is the word for man, and is the name of the first man (just as Adam is the English word for the name of the first man). There are many variations to the story of his creation, but the gist is very similar to the account given in Genesis. God (He is given several different names depending on the region or tribe that the story comes from, but we know that it is still God). He created man (Tiki or Adam) from earth or clay or dirt and then man became sad and lonely, so God created a wife for him out of his bones or ribs. They lived together in innocence until one day when his wife was tempted by an Eel (snake or serpent). She then tempted her husband (Tki or Adam) and they came together and procreated.

CHECK IT OUT! Read the Genesis account of creation and the fall and discuss how cultures around the world have a similar story of creation (even though they use different names to represent the characters in the story). We can know that scripture was not made up by one man or one group of men, when we learn that the history of cultures all over the world give the same account. List some other events that are historically common around the world (even in areas that have never had a Bible) and help us to know that Biblical history is accurate history.

FIND OUT! Tikis are wooden carvings that represent men of legend from mythology and folklore. These are graven images or idols that were once worshipped. (See the Ten Commandments in Exodus 20) What does God say about making graven images and worshipping idols?

Like the Totem Poles that are studied in Vacation Education destination Epcot, the purpose of the Tiki statues is to illustrate the story that is being passed on. These are especially common in the South Pacific area, like Hawaii. Most of the statues were left behind or destroyed when Christian missionaries arrived in Hawaii in 1820. Some of them have been uncovered and can be seen in museums as a representation of the culture's history.

TRY IT! Make a Tiki sculpture, not as a god or idol, but as a storytelling element. Using clay or Playdoh, sculpt a character of legend and use the sculpture to tell others a story about him. If the man had a big heart, sculpt a large heart shape onto his chest. If he was a martyr, sculpt a cross for him to carry to represent his commitment to Christ. Use this space to draw your Tiki design or to tell your story.

Today, the "Tiki" theme indicates a reference to Polynesian culture or design. See the Polynesian resort at Walt Disney World for a good example. The Tiki birds refer to the audio animatronic birds that have made this old temple ruin their home. The show itself is completely modern as it is now hosted by current movie characters Zazu and Iago.

Magic Carpets of Aladdin

Vocabulary

Aladdin

Morocco

Alan Menken

Howard Ashman

Morocco

The story line here is from the movie Aladdin; at the end of Aladdin, the magic lamp is thrown out with Jafar in it (his last wish was to be a Genie). However, the story goes that the lamp was recently discovered right here in Adventureland. There are many treasures to be found at your feet as elements of the land are embedded in the walkways. Can you find them and figure out where they came from? As you exit the ride, you are entering an area themed like the Morrocan marketplace... want to know more about this culture? Check out the Morocco pavilion at Epcot. (don't forget to pick up a copy of Vacation Education: destination Epcot.

In terms of rides, this one fits right in with Dumbo, they are essentially the same set up and attractive to the same generation. Aladdinsets you adrift on a magic carpet over the land of Agrabah. Watch out for spitting camels.

In terms of history and story, this is a better fit with fairy tales, myths and legends. Tales of lamps and genies have been around long enough to possibly compete with Beauty and the Beast for the title of tale as old as time.

The movie that inspired this attraction came from centuries old fairy tales. There are many variations available. Add this title to your list of fairy tales, myths and legends that you intend to study.

? DID YOU KNOW? Do you like the Soundtrack to Aladdin? This is another project by Menken and Ashman. You'll find their names come up a lot when people talk about great music and great movies.

The Magic Man
Making the Magic

This study covers three main ideas; the first is 'Walter' a unit that guides you through the story of a baby boy who would grow into the man responsible for pushing cinemagic into a future that others thought did not exist. 'Walter' will lead us into 'Mickey', his supposed alter ego. We will look at his progression from a mischievous little rat to the giant rodent everyone loves. Next, we will look from Walt's personal creation to those he influenced. From movies to park attractions, how did they come to be and why do they keep us coming back year after year? Let's Find Out!

 DID YOU KNOW? Walter Elias Disney was born on December 5, 1901. He passed away on December 15, 1966. Walt was the fourth of five children.

On October 16, 1923 Walter and Roy Disney began Disney Brothers studio. Their first production was Alice in Cartoon land. They would introduce the world to the first full length feature film done entirely in animation in 1937 with Snow White and the Seven Dwarfs.

DID YOU KNOW? Today, Disney Studios is the only major motion picture producer that does not run back lot tours.

Walt Disney World would not exist without its parent park Disneyland, which opened July 17, 1955. Walt designed and planned the Magic Kingdom, but died in December, 1966 before it was built. His brother Roy stepped up to help Walt's dream come true. The entire park is a story with pieces and parts all over the place. The goal of both Walt and the Imagineers of today is to bring each guest into that story. Every element tells a story, ask a cast member to tell you the tale.

Walt's first home was 1249 Tripp Avenue, Chicago, although he only lived there for a few years and considered Marceline, Missouri his home town. His parents encouraged him to pursue more practical career opportunities but he persisted in the art of cartooning. Some of his first jobs in animation involved advertisements that combined live actors with flat animated characters, like the Alice Comedies.

Walt and Roy were raised in a Christian family, and Walt was even named after their church's minister Walter Parr. Hid middle name came from his father Elias. When Disneyland opened, Walt invited Reverend Puder to deliver the invocation at the Grand Opening. Through his own words, he expressed his ideals, the power of prayer in his life, his reliance on God for all things, and a responsibility to produce films that were morally upright. He felt it was his duty to portray on film, not a world where there is only good, but a world where good always wins. This made the public appreciate his stories even more as the country suffered through the Great Depression and then WWII. Mickey Mouse is the character that brought Walt's artistic talent to the worlds' attention. His debut was in Steamboat Willie., and although he was a caricature of a mouse, his personality was that of every man. Even when others tried to cheat Walt or put pressure on him to sell out, he stood firm on Biblical principles that he believed were vital as an example to all children, his own in particular.

There are plenty of sources available for a study on Walt, Mickey and the history of their beginnings together. Walt did not invent the cartoon, or film or cameras or any of the elements that make movies work, but he was an artist who took risks on up and coming technology, using tools before many even knew they existed in order to stretch the possibilities in animation. He did produce the first complete cartoon with synchronized sound (Steamboat Willie) and the first full length feature film done completely in animation (Snow White and the Seven Dwarfs). His fame comes not only from his art but from his willingness to step out in faith with a new product and use it to its utmost capabilities, continuously wowing audiences.

CHECK IT OUT! From you local library. There are many, many books written about the man named Walt Disney. He has become something of an American folk hero. Look up Disney and choose at least two books to take home and learn more about this character in history. Here are a couple of suggestions, if you can find these; Fascinating Walt Disney by Stephen Schochet and Remembering Walt: Favorite Memories of Walt Disney by Amy Boothe Green and Howard E. Green.

 DID YOU KNOW? When the Disney company first began, it was called WED enterprises. The acronym stands for Walter Elias Disney.

TRY IT! Make a Timeline with all of the dates you discover as you read about Walt Disney's life. Here are a few dates to get your timeline started.

1901: At age 16, Walt quit school and joined the Red Cross, by 20 he was back in Kansas City making Laugh-o-Grams

1928: Walt produces Steamboat Willie (the first cartoon to be a 'talkie') with his character Mickey Mouse; have you heard of him? He's a pretty famous guy nowadays. Did you know his name was almost Mortimer? Walt's wife Lillian convinced him to change the mouse's name to Mickey.

1937: Snow White and the Seven Dwarfs hit theaters, the first full-length animated movie. We'll talk about dreaming big with this one, almost everyone told Walt he was wasting his time and money on this... no one would sit through an hour and a half cartoon, let alone pay for it.

1955: Disneyland opens in Anaheim, California. Walt, a family man, wanted to create a place where fathers could take their children and enjoy something together. Walt spent his Saturdays with his family and lamented that there weren't many options for activities that everyone could participate in. Disneyland was such a popular destination, that Walt decided to build an even bigger park, but he died in 1966 and never saw his dream come to fruition.

1971: Walt Disney World opens in Lake Buena Vista, Florida. Walt's brother Roy continued the building of this dream park. At opening, it consisted of only the Magic Kingdom. No other park since has had quite the impact as this one. When we mention Disney World, it's the Magic Kingdom that most people think of.

1975: Space Mountain opens. It was the first roller coaster at WDW.

1995 Toy Story is released by Disney/Pixar. This was the first film made entirely by CGI.

1996 WDW celebrates its 25th anniversary.

2001 With many box office hits to back up the decision, animated films were finally given a listing at the Oscars. What does it take to qualify for the Academy Award of Best Animated Feature Film? FIND OUT!

2002 100 year celebration of Disney magic. This represents one hundred years after Walt's birth.

2007 The first year of One Million Dreams.

> *"Mickey quickly became a phenomenon. ... I think it is because Mickey had a personality. Ub Iwerks and Walt Disney had created an every man, or a reflection of their culture. In 1928 this meant he was a wild, musical, scamp; willing to try anything. As the culture changed so did Mickey, and he remained a cultural touchstone until at least the middle of the next decade."*
> *Lee Suggs*

Walt was not the first to add animation to film. In 1909 Wiinsor McCay was performing on vaudeville stages with "Gertie, the Trained Dinosaur". The animated dinosaur appeared to respond to McCay's commands, and thrilled audiences. The next year, cartoons that told a story began to appear. Keep in mind though, at the time, films were still silent, so it was difficult to give animated characters much more than trick parts. In theaters, an orchestra or even an organ could be used to add music to the film.

During the 1920's Winkler Productions produced the most famous cartoons like 'Felix the Cat' and 'Out of the Inkwell'. They were also responsible for 'Alice Comedies' and "Oswald the Lucky Rabbit". "Alice" and "Oswald" were both products of Walt Disney Comics, but it was Winkler who controlled them.

✔ CHECK IT OUT! Watch an old Oswald cartoon. Does he look familiar to you? Some people think he looks a lot like a certain famous mouse. What do you think?

? DID YOU KNOW? 'Felix the Cat' was the only cartoon of the time that was really popular among movie goers, and even then, it was just a filler (like a pre-show act).

In 1928, Winkler cut Disney's payments for Oswald, and made secret deals to steal his animators. Disney was squeezed out. He was left with little choice, but to go on. He certainly wasn't the type to give up. He sketched out a new character on a train ride, and soon he and Ub had produced a short called "Plane Crazy". It flopped! It was silent and audiences found it to be very similar to the Oswald cartoons they'd already seen. Why buy an imitation Oswald if you can get the real thing? Walt had to come up with something different and do it quick.

Max Fleischer was experimenting with animation and sound effects with some success. Audiences dismissed the idea. Disney turned this idea over in his head and tried to make a deal with RCA and Western Electric. After some difficulties, he tried it out on his own. He finally recorded the soundtrack with a 15 piece band and his own voice for Mickey. He became the first animator to produce a cartoon complete with synchronized sound. It worked and brought people out in droves to see "Steamboat Willie".

As for Fleischer, he would go on to be the first animator to experiment with color in cartoons, and would prove to be tough competition for Disney in the 1930's and 1940's. He is famous for cartoons like "Superman", "Betty Boop", and "Popeye the Sailor Man".

DID YOU KNOW? Mickey's birthday is November 18, 1928. Walt maintained a hands on approach to the entire process of Steamboat Willie, including using his own voice for Mickey, and it was on November 18th, 1928 that it finally opened at he Colony Theater in New York.

CHECK IT OUT! Walt spent a lot of time in front of the media and therefore many of his words were recorded for history. He is famous for saying many things. Here are a couple of my personal favorites:

"A man should never neglect his family for business."

About his plans for Disneyland:

"We believed in our idea—a family park where parents and children could have fun—together."

Put your favorite Disney quote here:

CHECK IT OUT! As you browse through the shops, be on the lookout for some of the artisans hard at work here.

"We met a sketch artist from France working on the street, and a glass blower showing off his wares as well as his talents."

Remember to ask questions of these artists, they will be flattered at your interest in their career, and happy to show you how it is done.

"The Disney job I want to learn more about is the interpretive signers. Twice on our trip we saw the signers perform. I talked to one who said there were only six people in the whole place who could do the job she did. I love theater and think it would be a really fun job... plus, it sounds like they need people to do it."
S.J. Age 12

Before there could be jobs at WDW, there were a lot of jobs to be done. Ub Iwerks drew and animated the original Mickey Mouse. He was from Kansas City, Missouri. He grew up during the agricultural revolution while Kansas City was growing to an industrial mecca. Eert Iwerks (Ub's father) was an inventor in a time when there was a whole new world of film.

The job of the animators is to bring the drawings to life on film. Iwerk's father left when he was young. He became the breadwinner for his family, and quit school in order to go to work. Four years later, after educating himself and discovering a love of art and drawing, he enrolled at the Fine Arts Institute of Kansas City. He was just 18. As he worked, it was soon discovered that he had great talent. Pessman Ruben Commercial Arts Studio was his first employer as an artist. He soon met and made friends with another young artist named Walter. They found they had a lot in common and began "Iwerks-Disney", their own business offering advertising art. This was short lived and they quickly went back to work to earn a regular paycheck. They both found work at a Kansas City advertising agency, where they were paid to create commercials, but learned about the new and amazing technology of animation; bringing drawings to life on film.

They didn't give up, but borrowed a camera and created a comedy short for the Newman Theatre. They were soon hired to do a series of these short "Newman Laugh-O-Grams". While things might have been fun, it was not financially lucrative. Walt and Ub convinced their family and friends to invest more money, but even then the money soon ran out. These men were not willing to give up. Walt moved to California with little more than a few dollars and some cartoon sketches in his possession. He convinced his brother Roy to partner with him and opened the Disney Brothers Studio. Walt had great ideas, but he needed the artistic skills of Ub to make his ideas come to fruition. Ub packed up himself and his mother and followed Walt to California.

This group created "Alice in Cartoonland" and Oswald the Lucky Rabbit. Essentially, the idea of Oswald the Rabbit was stolen from Walt. His good friend Ub, informed him that he was being squeezed out of the deal and many of the animators that worked for him had already accepted job offers for better pay with Mintz. Ub not only stayed on with Walt, he singlehandedly took Walt's idea for a new mouse character and drew an entire film by himself behind closed doors, with no help, at a record setting speed of 700 drawings per day. Disneyland and Walt Disney World, and even Mickey Mouse are the brain children of Walt, but the actual creations of Mickey Mouse and the first cartoon, "Plane Crazy" (produced the same year that Lindbergh flew the Atlantic) was all due to Ub. Walt wrote the story lines, and the gags, while Ub drew the animation and brought the gags to life.

As Talkies were gaining popularity, Walt had the idea to make an animated film with sound. They did this by hiding behind a screen while the film ran and playing pot and pan instruments along with the actions. Walt wrote the story lines, Roy developed the financing, and Ub drew the animation. This team had finally, after much work and determination, created a concept that it seemed no competitor could top. Carl Stalling presented Walt with the idea of the Silly Symphony, going from trying to match sound to the completed animation, to instead using existing music and drawing a story around the musical piece. The most well known film of this type is Walt Disney's Fantasia. All of these ideas were done for the creative element, creating something for the art of it and sending it out in hopes that it would be a hit. No market testing was done, they weren't even sure who their target market would be.

They had no idea that Mickey Mouse would have worldwide appeal among all ages and races.

> ✓ CHECK IT OUT! Look for old newspaper articles, especially during war times, that refer to the effects of Mickey Mouse on the world.

? DID YOU KNOW? As Mickey became famous, Walt became famous, and Ub fell into the shadows, so while they had great respect for each other's work, Ub found the idea of setting out on his own a very attractive proposition. When the opportunity arose, he resigned from Disney Studios. Iwerks studios soon became the place to be for up and coming animators, as Ub was well known for producing work far superior to any one else in the field at the time. The creator of Betty Boop, and the animator for Bugs Bunny and Road Runner are just a sampling of the artists that leaned their trade from Ub.

Ub built the first three dimensional camera out of parts from an old Chevrolet. Several planes of drawings were used, so that the film appeared to have depth. Ub's technical skills and satire on real life, even though they were technically advanced, struggled to compete with Disney's simple cartoons with sympathetic story lines, which were more accepted by Americans struggling during the Depression.

Audiences were more interested in the characters that were being created by Disney, characters they could relate to, than they were interested in development of animation. Ub's biggest competitor was his own creation, Mickey Mouse; a character that audiences could identify with. Today, while good animation is important, the animated films are judged by audiences the same way live films are judged, the story and the characters.

Ub decided to close his doors and look for work. When Walt heard that Ub was available, he invited him back to Disney studios, knowing what a great asset his talents would be. So, Ub returned to Disney Studios. This gave Disney the edge in the field because Ub was always pushing the envelope of animation, revolutionizing the animation industry. He worked with Xerox to develop the process of copying the original drawings directly, skipping the necessity of inking (sometimes the inkers were amateur artists and the drawings would be changed slightly during this step).

 CHECK IT OUT! Watch 101 Dalmations and Mary Poppins to see some examples of the advances in animation made possible by Iwerks.

DID YOU KNOW? In the Alfred Hitchcock movie, "The Birds" when they tried to film it with real trained birds, they couldn't get them to attack the actors. The actors were then asked to respond to scripted bird attacks when the birds weren't really even there. Ub Iwerks made it possible for this film to be made, adding in the animated birds later on.

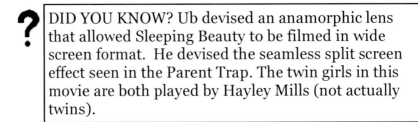 **DID YOU KNOW?** Ub devised an anamorphic lens that allowed Sleeping Beauty to be filmed in wide screen format. He devised the seamless split screen effect seen in the Parent Trap. The twin girls in this movie are both played by Hayley Mills (not actually twins).

From 360 degree films to the first animatronics like Abraham Lincoln, and the seemingly life like ghosts in the Haunted Mansion; the work that Ub did laid the groundwork for the realistic believable animated films we have today where we often forget that we are watching cartoon characters.

History of Animation and Film
From humble beginnings to 3D theaters

Vocabulary

Animation

Technicolor

Herbert Kalmus

Kinemacolor

The Gulf Between

Toll of the Sea

Paramount

Wanderer of the Wasteland

The Black Pirate

Animation cameras were regular motion picture cameras that were adapted to be able to shoot stop film. Today, we think of animation as purely cartooning, but the first real use for these cameras was to creat special effects. The cameraman would take a shot of an object, stop the camera, move it, and take another shot. In hand drawn animation, the same kind of camera is still used, although today's technology is so advanced that movies go straight from computer software to DVD (digital video disk).

Technicolor is the brand name of a company ran by Herbert Kalmus and his wife Natalie. Although, they made color what it is today, they didn't invent the idea. Kinemacolor was the first successful color motion picture process. In the early 1900's, they produced a two color additive process, photographing on black and white film and then projecting it with red and green filters.

Technicolor put color in the film. They were able to dye the film to produce the colors, which made them richer and more realistic. They basically split the film strip in half and dyed one piece red and the other green, and then put them back together to make a strip of film that would fit into the cameras that motion picture mak-

 FIND OUT! What was the name of the first feature film to be produced in Technicolor? Do you think it's Wizard of Oz?

Kalmus produced "The Gulf Between" using this two color technology for the purpose of trying to sell the concept to movie producers. They weren't terribly impressed, but a few movie-goers saw bits of color start to appear in films such as "Toll of the Sea" (1922-23). Paramount agreed to allow Kalmus to film "Wanderer of the Wasteland" in color with the concession that they wouldn't spend any extra time or money on it. While this film saw some success, movie-goers were not overly impressed and movie makers were not convinced that they should pursue the technology.

While trying to sell their idea, Technicolor continued to make improvements and soon introduced a 2nd Process, which was visibly better in quality. Several movies would use the color process in a few scenes but otherwise keep the movie black and white. In 1926 Douglas Fairbanks produced a big budget film entirely in color. The Black Pirate was successful but the fame went to Fairbanks more than Technicolor, and the public was not demanding color, so movie producers were still unwilling to pay more for it.

Kalmus continued to make improvements and the 3rdProcess made the film much easier to use, and more convenient. In 1928, MGM produced the VIKING, the first feature film to use both color and sound. By 1930, color was gaining ground as Warner Brothers produced nearly a dozen full color feature films, but by 1931, the Depression had slowed down the movie making industry. Theaters saw less patrons, and those who did attend were more interested in being able to hear the voices of the actors and actresses than they were in knowing what color their clothes were.

In 1932, Technicolor introduced Process 4. This was a three-strip film that didn't require being taken apart and put back together. This meant that filmmakers could use it without having the expense of time and money spent waiting for it to be shipped to Kalmus to be processed. Kalmus hired a machinist to build the first three-strip camera.

In 1928, Walt Disney had taken a big risk, financially and artistically by producing Steamboat Willie with a soundtrack. It was risky, but innovative, and that was the kind of producer that Technicolor needed. While other motion picture companies were focused on profits, Walt's focus was on raising enough money to make improvements and to take on the next challenge. Kalmus approached Disney with the New Technicolor Process, and Walt loved it. He negotiated a contract for exclusive use, and produced Silly Symphonies—Flowers and Trees, and shortly thereafter The Three Little Pigs.

> ✔ CHECK IT OUT! Disney has a reputation for taking a story we already know and putting his art into it. The story itself is not his creation, but the storytelling is. Disney's early films stick to a moral guideline of right is right and wrong is wrong, which Walt was known for. Take the time to view Disney films such as Father Noah's Ark and Johnny Appleseed.

How is it that much of the country struggled near to starvation during the Depression, but Walt's company continued to flourish and his staff increased?

What does this say about the priorities of our culture?

In times of great need, we turn to cartoon antics on television to escape the reality of our need for God's saving grace?

Perhaps it is the fun in film like the Three Little Pigs that helped people to escape from the reality of the Depression. What do you suppose was the country's most popular song at the time?

"Who's Afraid of the Big Bad Wolf?"

Around 1934, Walt began preparations for Snow White, although he'd had the story in his head for quite some time. Theaters paid for minutes, not popularity or quality. He needed to produce a feature film for the money it would bring his company, but he wanted to make one for the challenge it brought him personally. Others scoffed, saying that it couldn't be done, no one would watch it, and it would cost too much money to be worthwhile.

FIND OUT! In the past few years, how many full-length feature films have been released that are mostly or entirely animated? Shrek! Madagascar! Ratatouille! Veggie Tales! How many people do you think went to see those films?

Walt's critics said no one would sit and watch a cartoon for an hour and a half!

One major challenge for the animators working on Snow White was drawing her movements. Everyone in the audience would have a presupposed idea of what a woman's movements should look like. Unlike characters such as Mickey whose movements could be awkward, to make a human character believable, nothing could be guessed. It would have to be accurate. They hired actress Marge Champion to play out the scenes on film, and then drew the characters from that footage.

Another challenge was the outdoor nature scenes. How do you draw a rainstorm on paper, take a picture of it, and have it look like a real rainstorm on the big screen? How do you make waterfalls appear to be actually moving?

  TRY IT! Make your own animated film. Write a script, draw the characters and scenes, use a video camera (today's technology makes this a much simpler process than Disney had when he first started) to put your ideas from paper to film.

When you have it complete, show it to your friends.

You can use a digital camera, and send it to others on your computer also.

Or make a slide show in a power point type program.

Use any medium available that your comfortable using.

If you've never used any of this technology, take this opportunity to find someone who has and learn from them.

📖 FIND OUT! Learn how a digital or video camera works. How is it the same or different than the one that Disney used to film Snow White and the Seven Dwarfs? Technicolor's three strip camera became the benchmark for future productions, and many tried in vain to copy their process.

Is this still true today?

Does current technology keep improving on Kalmus's concept, or have they come up with something different?

It didn't take long for other filmmakers to see the potential that Disney had seen in color films, and they put pressure on Kalmus for access to the new technology. Disney managed to keep exclusive rights to the process for animation only. In 1935, "Becky Sharp" starring Miriam Hopkins debuted as the first full length live action film entirely in Technicolor. One year later, 'Trail of the Lonesome Pine' would be the first color production to be filmed on location instead of in a light controlled studio, and everyone was pleasantly surprised by the results. Imagine being able to film actual mountains instead of trying to replicate them inside a building.

As for the Wizard of Oz? Well, MGM was a little behind other filmmakers on the color wagon, but when they did it in 1939, they did it with a bang! Most people still think that the transition of black and white Kansas to vibrant and colorful Munchkinland was the introduction of Technicolor. It may not have been the first, but it was certainly the movie that brought full color capabilities to the attention of the viewing public.

✋ TRY IT! Pull out the photos from your last trip, or if this is your first, get together with friends who have been, and look at their photos. Imagine that Disney has just hired you to create a brochure for them to entice people to visit their parks. You can use the photos that you already have or take new ones on your next trip just for this purpose. What will you include?
(Creative Art) (Graphic Design)
(Career Exploration-Advertising/

✓ CHECK IT OUT! From your local library. Search for a book on the subject of Walt Disney and animation. We found "The Art of Walt Disney" by Christopher Finch available in most libraries we checked, and it was a fascinating read.

TRY IT! Put together your own television show. Using techniques you've learned in your study, write a script for an animated or live production. Film your production and show it to your friends and family.
(Writing) (Life Skills) (Computers/ Technology) (Public Speaking)

TRY IT! Create a slide show of your Disney Vacation, or of your virtual world vacation (if you're doing Epcot also). Present this at a senior home or for another group that might be unable to travel, but would enjoy seeing the sights
(Community Speaking) (Computer skills) (Photography)
(Community Service)

TRY IT! Create a music and dance video for your favorite song.

   The first two films about Mickey Mouse were silent. In Steamboat Willie, Walt Disney decided to take a chance with sound. He created a story that would need sound effects that went along with the story. His competitors said he was wasting time and money. Who would ever believe that sound could come from a cartoon drawing? Walt believed. He hired an orchestra to play the sound track along with a bouncing ball he filmed in the lower corner. Even though we now have the ability to record sound along with the action, many sound effects are still added afterwards.

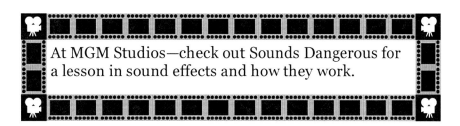

At MGM Studios—check out Sounds Dangerous for a lesson in sound effects and how they work.

TRY IT! Make a silent movie, then create a taped soundtrack to go with it.
   Things sound different on tape than they do in your presence. A real door slamming would sound like a gun shot on tape, but two boards clapped together might make a more realistic sounding door slam. Experiment with different objects to make the most realistic soundtrack you can.
(Creative design) (Science/Technology) (Exploration of Environment)

Animation has changed over the years, and many of the advancements in filming come from the ability to computer generate images. Walt Disney created animation by drawing the characters every movement by hand. Pixar uses computers. Can you tell the difference? The first film that was completely computer animated was Toy Story.

CHECK IT OUT! Find a recent film created through traditionally drawn animation. Find a film produced by computer animation. What are the differences? Watch the two movies together with some friends and family and discuss the pros and cons of each method. Prepare some questions in advance based on your study of animation to use as conversation starters.
(Leadership) (Public Speaking) (Analytical debate) (Logic)

Link to MGM Studios:

The Back Lot Tour at MGM gives you a chance to walk through some exhibits of old props, leading to the preshow, where you could be chosen to come on stage and help teach the audience how special effects are done in a boat scene. After this, you board a tour bus that takes you past homes of the stars, okay not their actual homes, but the houses that were used on screen for the shows they were in. You'll also get a glimpse into a real costuming department (this is most active during the day, in the evening you may not actually see anyone at work there). It is the largest working costume department anywhere, providing costumes for movies made all over the world.

At the Animation Gallery, you can see the awards won by Walt Disney. He earned 32 Academy Awards, way more than any other producer. The film in this attraction 'Magic of Disney Animation' begins with a presentation from Mushu, the dragon friend of Mulan. It used to include a real working animation studio where artists could be seen working on Disney's next film. This area was eliminated when most animation went to computer generated, and the exhibit has been replaced with a museum like model of an animators work station. Moving past this to the lower level, you can try some inking of your own on computers. You'll also have a chance to record your voice singing some Disney favorites, or to take a quiz to see which character you are most like.

At the top of the stairs is the entrance to a ten-minute drawing class, that begins every half-hour. It offers a quick overview of the method used to sketch a specific character.

"The schedule set up is such that it allows for time after class to ask questions of the instructor. This proved very beneficial for our son, who wanted the class to go on and on. You can of course get back in line and do it again."

Back at MGM, you'll find an attraction called, "ONE MAN"S DREAM". Follow a young sketch artist hired to draw cartoon antics to entertain audiences until the real show began on a journey to become a producer of films who can claim more Academy Awards than any other. His adventure continues as he goes on to create live action/animation combination films and then to be the designer of the parks that allow you to step inside his stories.

From here, make your way back to the Sorcerers Hat, and step inside the Chinese Theater. The real one is located at 6925 Hollywood Boulevard and may have had as many visitors as the one in Orlando. The structure in MGM is a replica of this Hollywood landmark where movie stars have been leaving their mark (literally) on the sidewalk for decades. Apparently, this tradition began when the owner invited celebrities to tour the new theater and an actress named Norma Talmadge accidentally stepped into some new cement.

The theater in Hollywood still shows movies, and you can get a look at the inside for about $10, the cost of a movie ticket. The replica in MGM houses, appropriately, the Great Movie Ride. You can see scenes from Mary Poppins, Indiana Jones, Singing in the Rain, Fantasia, Alien, Casablanca and more in the queuing area. As these thirty second shots come across the screen, you will recognize them if you have ever seen the movies.

FIND OUT! How is it that trailers or preview scenes are chosen? Who decides which clips will stick in a viewers mind, and make them want to see the rest of the movie? How do they make this decision?

TRY IT! Rent a few of these movies and watch them, keeping in mind the scene that was chosen for the clip. Why do you think they made the choice they did? Would you have made the same choice? Why or why not?(Creative Art) (Analytical Thinking)

CHECK IT OUT! See Mickey's Philharmagic at the Magic Kingdom. It's in 3-D!

TRY IT! Choose a recent movie, something computer animated and read several reviews for it. Then, choose a recent live-action film and read reviews for that. It doesn't matter which movies you choose. The point here is to analyze the different points of view. Even though the public can see both films and decide directly which they like better, you'll find that critics aren't looking at the same things. In animation, they are reviewing art and design, textures and movements; in live action, they are looking at the actors, the setting, props and directors ideas. Both forms should be judged on plot, scenery, sound and script. Once you have completed your analysis and have a feel for the requirements of a good review, select a third movie, animation or live action and write your own review for it. (Modern art) (Computer technology) (Logic) (non-fiction writing) (Critical thinking)

Three-dimensional films work by using the amazing technology of the human brain. Your two eyes work together to view the world from two different but similar angles and your brain puts the two images together into one scene.

TRY IT! To illustrate the above concept, find an item wide enough to extend past your view on both sides, such as a row of windows or a row of houses. Looking straight ahead at the middle of this view, cover one eye and then the other. Each time, count the number of houses or windows that you can see without moving your head. And compare that to the number you can see with both eyes open. This same concept comes into play when you use a Viewfinder toy, your eyes see two pictures and melds them together in your brain to see one consistent image. Three-dimensional movies work by using this fascinating aspect of your mind.

"The Lord knit me together in my mothers womb"

Two cameras shoot two different images at the screen and if you watch the film without the glasses it appears blurry, and not three dimensional. But, the glasses force each eye to see an image from just one camera and your brain puts the two together. By manipulating the shapes and size of objects in relation to each other, the images fool your brain into putting the two together and seeing part of the image on the screen and part as off the screen

SPOILER WARNING! SPOILER WARNING! SPOILER WARNING!

If you do not want to be spoiled, do not read until after your trip!

EPCOT: In Honey, I shrunk the Audience, currently playing in Future World, Imagineers have added the sensation of touch to the visual experience. Sprayers in the backs of the seats cause water to squirt at your face at the same time a huge dog is slobbering. Yuck!

Animal Kingdom: In It's Tough To Be a Bug, currently showing at The Tree of Life in Animal Kingdom, you can add several other sensations. Speakers in the seats allow you to hear bees buzzing in your ears, and blowers allow you to feel the wind from the insects wings. You can also smell the lovely odor of the stink-bug, and feel the cockroaches crawling along your back and legs as they exit the theater. In the words of one child, it's *Even Yuckier!*

Theater and Drama
Focus on Live Entertainment

Many of the stage shows take the form of musicals, showcasing the wonderful sound-tracks that have come from Disney's movies. What tactics do they use to keep people from rushing off to get in line for the next big thrill ride? This is especially relevant to street shows, as opposed to scheduled shows that you plan to sit and watch. There is no available schedule for much of the entertainment you will find on the corners of Disney streets. They call this the streetmosphere, and it just kind of happens as part of the theming. Pay attention to the tactics that the entertainers (cast members) use to get audience members involved.

"No matter how many times we visit Walt Disney World, the streetmosphere that we run across makes every trip different."

TRY IT! Prepare for this unit study by making a list of the things that you hope to learn from this unit study, and use it to create a questionnaire that you can fill out after you've seen some of the entertainment. Be sure to include questions that evaluate the differences between street shows and theater productions.

At MGM, Look for a car that looks like duct tape might be the only thing holding it together. It will say Hollywood Public Works on the side. When you find it, you'll be in for a treat. From inside this car, appear three guys who make fun of city workers, union breaks, and pretty much spend the entire show time throwing toilet plungers at a board. This is an example of streetmosphere, as it is not a scheduled show, but more like you just catch them at work (but not really working). You will most likely catch them behind Keystone Clothiers, an upscale clothing shop on Hollywood Boulevard.

TRY IT! Kiosks around MGM studios offer several options of special effects makeup for you. For a fee, you can get made up like one of many creatures from your favorite movies.

Everything at MGM Studios is about the movies beginning with the stroller rental at the entrance. It is themed as an old gas and service station. It's not a scene from any movie you'd recognize, but is a typical service station from the 1940's, and combined with the 1947 Buick parked out front, it brings you back in time to Hollywood's height of glamour.

The old cinema is currently home to displays supported by Kodak, including cameras, batteries and film for sale (just in case you forgot yours). The shops retail items are typical Disney fare, miscellaneous items with character's pictures on them. But, if you can see past the shelves filled with commercialism to the architecture and design of the building, there is much here to be appreciated. For instance, the walls of the five and dime are lined with photos of famous movie stars whose glamorous on screen lives provided entertainment and a sense that opportunities were still alive and well somewhere out there during the hard times of the 1930's and 1940's.

At Adrian and Edith's, you'll find personalized gifts to make you feel like a star. Once again, you have to look up and over the store shelves to see the best part, the movie costuming from a bygone era. You can purchase a name badge here just like a cast member and the store-keeper will engrave your name on it. But watch out, park guests might mistake you for the real thing and expect you to give them directions.

At the corner of Sunset and Highland stands the Carthay Circle Theater where Snow White and the Seven Dwarfs was originally shown. Like many of the structures in Disney World, it is used as a gift shop, but the architectural design is authentic and can still be appreciated.

Keep on down Sunset Boulevard until it ends at the entrance to the Hollywood Tower Hotel. Although not a real hotel, it was inspired by some of the famous ones in California. The exterior, gardens and other structural details came from hotels like The Mission Inn, The Biltmore, and Chateau Marmont. The theming, while obviously straight from The Twilight Zone, fits quite appropriately with the Hollywood Roosevelt Hotel. The Tower (storyline) was built in 1923 as a glamorous luxury hotel, but was abandoned in 1939 after a fateful lightning storm struck it, sending several guests and a bellhop into the Twilight Zone, never to be seen again.

The Roosevelt has its own ghost stories to tell. The most famous ghost is that of Marilyn Monroe who is said to appear in a hallway mirror that once adorned a room she often stayed in. Guests also claim they can hear Montgomery Clift pacing the floor and playing his bugle in a room he once used while shooting a movie nearby. The hotel is home to many not-so-famous haunts as well. Personally, I think the Hollywood Tower Hotel looks an awful lot like the Roosevelt.

Even if you skip out before you get on the elevator, I think it would be worth your while to walk the queuing area of this attraction. The attention to detail is exactly what you would expect from Disney.

If you didn't know better, you might actually believe you were standing in a real hotel from the 30's and that everyone had just up and walked away leaving it as it stands today. Pay close attention to the details. If you could find something that didn't fit, the whole thing would stop being believable. Take note of the aspects of this scene that you can transfer to your own use of theater. How do you take something fantastical and make it appear to be part of reality? What details are needed to really make a scene convincing?

Heading back up Sunset Boulevard, check your show schedule and plan to see the Beauty and the Beast stage production. This is a musical with very few props, and unlike the Hollywood Tower Hotel where props are the integral ingredient for drawing you into the illusion, here they rely more on costumes and music.

Pay attention to lighting changes.

How do they affect the overall production?

What is important about the timing of the lights?

Why is flash photography not allowed?

What affects do the lights have on the actors? What affects do the lights have on the audience?

FIND OUT & TRY IT! Want to know how a theater production really works? Volunteer to help out backstage at your local auditorium or theater. You can learn to create scenes, special effects, lighting and more. See how a dress rehearsal works. You can also volunteer to usher and see the

CHECK IT OUT! Read some of the plays written by William Shakespeare, and then watch them live or on video. Speak with your parents about which ones are appropriate for your age, and ask them to help you understand some of the language. These were originally written to be performed in outdoor arenas and props would have been few, so the author had to rely on the words and actions of the actors to tell the story.

FIND OUT! There are different kinds of stages. Some are designed for large productions and some are specifically designed to serve a small cast. How are they different? Make a list of the pros and cons of each type.

Details, details, details! We can learn a great deal about how to put on good theater from a master at it. Disney started out to become the best at cartoon animation, and it was his attention to details and his ability to stick with a project until it was perfect that made his success. Another master at theater is Cirque du Soleil. If you've never seen them in action, this is a can't miss event; Loa Nouba performs Downtown Disney. If the price of tickets steer you away from this production, don't fret. We have often caught them on television, and video tapes of their shows are available as well. The experience would not be the same, but the price is more attractive.

TRY IT! Join a theater group or start your own, perhaps in your church or school Learn to work a production from beginning to end. Starting with the writing of the script all the way to deciding who gets the flowers after the last performance
Alternative: Audition for a part in a theater production at your local church or school.

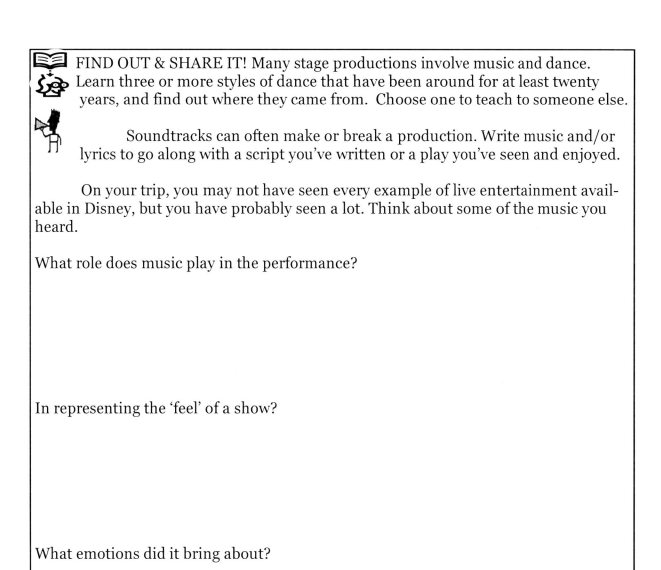

FIND OUT & SHARE IT! Many stage productions involve music and dance. Learn three or more styles of dance that have been around for at least twenty years, and find out where they came from. Choose one to teach to someone else.

Soundtracks can often make or break a production. Write music and/or lyrics to go along with a script you've written or a play you've seen and enjoyed.

On your trip, you may not have seen every example of live entertainment available in Disney, but you have probably seen a lot. Think about some of the music you heard.

What role does music play in the performance?

In representing the 'feel' of a show?

What emotions did it bring about?

At Magic Kingdom, the streetmosphere is ever present. Throughout the day, several performers roam the shopping district of Main Street. They are not on an official schedule, so your events guide might not even mention them.

"We tried asking at guest services and they couldn't even give us a list of characters to look for."

So, here is a sample list of some of the live entertainment that we have found. This is not necessarily an exhaustive list, but it will at least give you a list to begin a scavenger hunt to find them all. Of course, if you discover some that we missed, we'd love to hear from you. You can contact us through our website: vacationeducationbooks.com

Fantasyland: There are daily performances on the castle stage.
    Fantasyland Woodwind Society
    Belle's Story time
    Mickey's Toon Town Tuners
Frontierland:
    Notorious Banjo Brothers and Bob
    Country Bear Jamboree (not exactly live, but on stage)
    Woody's Cowboy Camp
Adventureland:
    Captian Jack Sparrow's Pirate Tutorial
Main Street:
    Dapper Dans Barbershop Quartet
    Casey's Pianist
    Flag Retreat (Daily in Town Square)
    Hot Time Trio
    Main Street Philharmonic
    Trolley Parade
    Opening Ceremony (Daily at entrance)
Tomorrowland:
    PUSH, the Talking Trashcan

Throughout the day, there are character greetings in every area of the parks.

"We enjoyed the Dapper Dans barbershop quartet and the pianist at Casey's Corner"

"Our children were fascinated by the glass blower at Arribas as we watched him create fragile souvenirs…"

"The most memorable moments for us came from seeing artists at work. Where much of Disney is fantasy, these were real."

"The Main Street Philharmonic plays daily in Town Square and is a performance you won't want to miss."

"We have also found cast members playing games outside guest services. … We joined them for hoola hooping and jump roping at Magic Kingdom [popular games of the time period] and watched a man make balloon animals that the kids got to keep at Epcot."

TRY IT! Write a short skit for an animated film. Rewrite the script for a stage production.
What alterations do you need to make for it to work?

TRY IT & SHARE IT! Overhead projection screens and slide shows are a common part of many presentations and dramas. They are even used in many churches today. Learn to create and present a slide show with Power Point or similar software. If you already know how, teach someone else.

TRY IT & SHARE IT! Create an educational film on video tape showcasing some of the activities you've done, places you've seen and things you've learned from this unit study. You could use this as your final exam for the unit or as a record of the study.

Main Street U.S.A.
Map

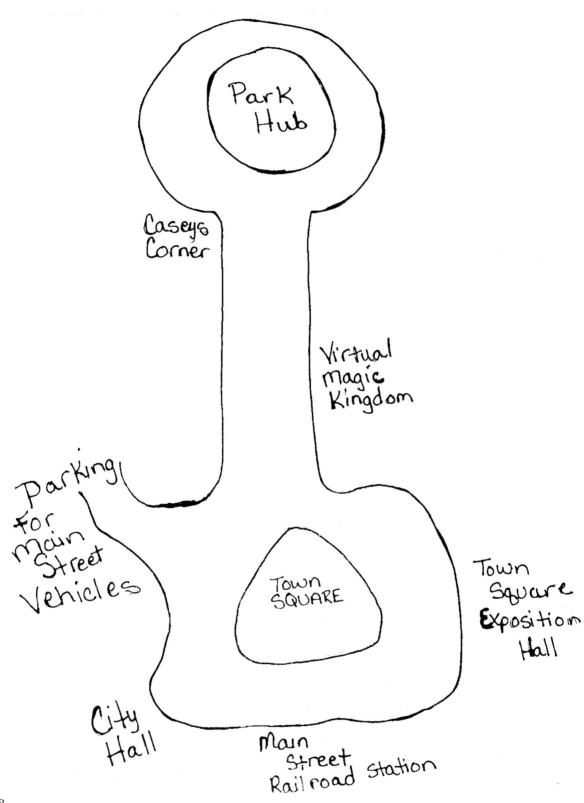

Park Hub

Caseys Corner

Virtual magic Kingdom

Parking for main Street Vehicles

Town SQUARE

Town Square Expositiom Hall

City Hall

Main Street Railroad Station

Main Street, U. S. A.

Vocabulary

Architecture

Marceline, Missouri

Blue print

Colonial

Bavarian

Pagoda

Franklin automobile

Streetmosphere

Proprieter

Forced perspective

Begin your journey into the world of Disney on the street designed like Walt remembered his turn of the century home town of childhood days. The setting here is inspired by the real life town of Marceline, Missouri and representative of 1890-1910 architecture. Pay close attention to the theming inside the shops, particularly the walls and ceilings. The most obvious is the architecture, which stays the same no matter how often the store's contents are changed. But, by looking up as you walk through, you can spot things most people miss. For example, in the Emporium Gallery, near the ceiling you'll find a display of items that would have been for sale in such a shop in the early 1900's.

CHECK IT OUT! Main Street Train Station: Find the plaques in the train station that explains each person's importance in the creation of the Magic Kingdom. The names of the trains are Lilly Belle (Walt's wife), Walter E. Disney, Roy O. Disney, Roger E. Braggie. There is a shelf here with passenger luggage waiting to be loaded on board. From the contents, can you guess who your traveling companions are?

The Walt Disney World Rail Road begins at the Town Square on Main Street. You have to walk under the station to enter the park. The track travels one and one half miles around the park, making two stops; one at Frontier land and the other at Toon Town Fair. This railroad was inspired by Walt's days as a sales boy for the Santa Fe RR.

DID YOU KNOW? There is capacity for 100,000 people to fit inside these gates at one time. Sometimes, the park actually gets that full!

Streetmosphere means that everything stays in character; even the shops. The Emporium is much like a department store and even the proprieter (who no one has ever actually seen and as far as we know is currently un-named) has a story of his personal and business success. See if you can find out the details.

Can you find the credits? The entire production is a show, and every show has credits. Walt made sure to put them in a prominent location. Along Main Street, and other areas throughout the parks, you can see the names of business owners printed on the glass of the storefronts. Jot down some of these names, and then see if you can find out what important role they played in the design and development of the Magic Kingdom. Check out such businesses as the Cinema, the Old Fashioned candy store, and the Arribas Brothers glass blowers.

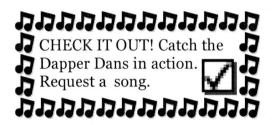

CHECK IT OUT! Catch the Dapper Dans in action. Request a song.

TRY IT! Document your home town. Take photos of community events, and see if your local newspaper, or chamber of commerce has a use for them. Smaller papers do not have enough staff to cover all newsworthy events. Write an article to go with your photo, and you may have a profitable venture.

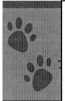

CHECK IT OUT! 'Tony' of Tony's Town Square Restaurant is famous as the restauranteer who served spaghetti to Lady and the Tramp. Look outside for the paw prints.

"Throughout the park, there are places to sit and relax over a game of checkers. This is one of the last things we do before we leave. There is a board outside Tony's Town Square Restaurant. We like to stop here for just a few minutes on our way out before we say goodbye to the park."

TRY IT! Study the different types of architecture that were popular around the turn of the century (1800's to 1900's). The dictionary definition is "...the art and science of designing buildings and structures." Look for examples of styles of architecture in your town so that you can recognize them. When you get to the Magic Kingdom, look for examples of the kinds of architecture you studied.

CHECK IT OUT! Find out what type of architecture your home is. Draw a blue print of it. Make design changes. If you had been the original architect, what would you have done differently? Draw a second blueprint of it showing the changes. How many different types of architecture can you identify in Magic Kingdom?

FIND OUT! Choose an architectural style that you particularly like and learn how an architect would have designed it. Draw a picture of it and make a scale model of it. This does not have to be limited to American colonial period, but can include adobe huts like in Adventure Land, or Bavarian Alps like in Germany and Fantasy Land or even the pagodas in Japan and the eight tiered one that houses the Tiki bird show.

TRY IT! Take photographs of homes in your neighborhood. Ask the owners if they know when it was built or any of its history. Make a timeline of the construction on your street. Do you see any patterns? Was all the growth at once or over a long period? Did an economic boom help your town grow? Did a slump slow it down? Compare the oldest homes with the most recent—how is the architecture different? For example: one community might have a neighborhood of Victorian homes all built during a lumbering boom, another neighborhood of cookie cutter homes built for young families right after a war, a trailer park from the 80's when real estate slumped, and so on.

FIND OUT! Can you find examples of forced perspective? Don't know what to look for?
It's a trick on your eyes that makes a two story tall building appear to be three or more stories. It can work the other way too. See any examples now?

The early 1900's are full of adventure all their own, new technology, hope for the future, plenty of jobs for everyone, wealth abounding, plenty of new inventions and plenty of money to buy them. Horse drawn carriages share the streets with motor vehicles, showing the changing of the times.

If you are looking for someone specific in the neighborhood, the odd numbered addresses are on the left and evens are on the right (as you enter the park). Making your way down Main Street, take note of the names in the windows, like Earl Vilmer, Ron Miller and Roy Disney, to name a few. Then, go to the Emporium and view the streetscape painting on the wall. The people pictured here match the names on the windows. These details blend into the surroundings, but are actually a tribute to the people who helped make Main Street, USA possible. It is their names and faces that are depicted here.

The Main Street Cinema used to show movies; old Disney cartoons actually, but now is home to the virtual kingdom. The technology for this game has overtaken the building, but if you look closely, the original details are still there. In all of the Main Street structures, you must look up overhead to see the pieces of history that tell the shopkeeper's story. Be assured that in step with Disney fashion, everything is part of a story.

At Casey's Corner, catch a tune from the turn of the century as the shop's pianist plays outside. Inside, take a break in air conditioning while you watch old black and white Disney cartoons from the stadium style seating (literally bleachers) . The surrounding theme here is baseball, the American pastime.

If all this shopping makes you feel like you must buy something, look for the practical purchases. There are many Disney themed items that are more than cutesy souvenirs, but are useful too.

"I have a Mickey Mouse chef's apron and a S&P shaker set that I just love"

> **?** DID YOU KNOW? The woman in the ticket booth at the Main Street Cinema was modeled after Walt's wife Lillian?

> **?** DID YOU KNOW? The tickets in the booth here are the original park tickets.

In the Town Square, at the end of Main Street is the history of Disney animation theater. Go all the way through this building to find some special treasures in the back. There are several opportunities for great fun photos, like aboard a spaceship with the little green aliens from Buzz Lightyear or picture yourself on TV as a favorite star to the Dalmation Pups. Plenty of informative material as well. We found its often not crowded and is a nice place to let little ones enjoy some of Disney's originals in this movie theater. Also, a quiet air conditioned spot to nurse an infant while enjoying a cute movie.

"We love to hang out in the back of the cinema, watch some classic Disney cartoons, and get our pictures taken in the funny scenes. We often get to see characters coming and going from the break room just off the theater too."

Main Street, USA exemplifies the dawn of the Industrial Revolution, homes have both gas lamps and electric bulbs. The road is shared by horseless carriages and horse-drawn trollies, guests can use all of these modes of transportation, taking a ride on the horse drawn trolley or in an old fashioned car (also referred to as a jitney), or the Antique Fire Engine. Board at the Town Square or at Cinderella's Castle. Pick up a copy of the transportation schedule at City Hall.

CHECK IT OUT! For horse lovers—You can say hello to the horses on their break by visiting them at the Car Barn by the Emporium.

DID YOU KNOW? The horses live at Fort Wilderness and have plastic horse-shoes (they are easier on the hooves than metal)

 Here's an idea for a unit study: The invention of the automobile. The cars featured here are models of the Franklin automobile from 1903 to 1907 with a 4 cylinder Hercules gasoline engine.

FIND OUT! As you study different types of architecture, see if you can find examples of Eastern Seaboard Victorian on Main Street.

CHECK IT OUT! Visit the Main Street Firehouse and look for a badge from your hometown. These badges have been donated from real working fire houses all over the country and are displayed here to honor them. If you don't see one from your hometown; ask a cast member where to send one and see if your local firehouse will donate one to add to the display. While you're at it, plan a field trip to your local firehouse to see how things work and to thank the men and women for the job that they do.

 DO YOU KNOW? How it is that the music and characters, announcer, etc. are all perfectly in sync no matter where you are when you watch them go by in the parade? There are sensors in the road way that signal a computer system as the float passes by. This is also used to keep all the floats in line and the correct distance apart.

Transportation

This chapter is filled with activities that you can do at home with very little expense. Young children tend to be very interested in vehicles, like big trucks, fire engines, police cars, and trains. This unit has activities for every age group. It also contains activities that can be done in any other parks, or in just one.

Don't forget about the vocabulary words. When you are reading on your own or checking out a website, be sure to add words that you find there to your list. These serve several purposes; not only to increase your vocabulary (essential for high SAT scores), but can also be used a spelling lists, further research ideas, and lead ins to new unit studies.

CHECK IT OUT! The basic modes of transportation are land, sea, and air. How many different kinds of transportation can you think of? Start three lists with the headings land, sea or air, and add to the list as you work on this unit. Some suggestions to get you started are ferry boats, mountain bikes, horse drawn wagons, and canoes.

Your feet are a kind of transportation and the kind you use most often. Disney parks require a lot of walking, and that combined with the heat makes for rapid dehydration. Plan to drink plenty of fluids on your trip.

 FIND OUT! What are the symptoms of dehydration?

List them here:

144

TRY IT! Start walking every day, at least a few blocks, and try to go a little farther each day. While you're enjoying the Disney parks, you probably won't even notice how many miles you walk each day. But, the more you prepare, the less often you'll need to take a break and the more sights you'll get to see. Besides, walking every day is a really good habit to start, so see if you can keep it up after you return home from your trip.

Challenge Yourself: Make a chart showing the distance you travel and the time you spend on your walk. Each day, challenge yourself to walk farther in the same period of time or to walk for a longer period of time. Ask other family members to make a chart also, and see who improves the most after a designated period of time (like thirty or ninety days).

Most accidents are due to human error, whether it is in a car, on a bicycle or at an amusement park. What can you do to help others protect themselves and make the world safer for you and those around you? Make a list here and then choose one to try.

CHECK IT OUT! Take a walk to a place where you can see stop signs, traffic signals, and other safety signs. Discuss what each of these means. When you get home, using index cards or similar, draw a picture of each sign that you remember, and a picture of yourself doing what the sign tells you to do. You can use these drawings later to play a matching game to reinforce the safety signals that you have learned.

CHECK IT OUT! & SHARE IT! Choose a type of transportation and look up current safety information and products. Can you suggest possible improvements to existing materials? Create a presentation of your ideas.

 TRY IT! Put together an emergency kit for traveling. Would it contain the same items if you were traveling by bicycle as if you were traveling by place. Make a list of items that you would put in an emergency kit for several different types of transportation. Then, actually make one to take on your trip to Disney. How are you traveling? What will you need?

TRY IT! Play red light/green light. One person is the traffic light, and when they say green light, all the other players run towards him. When he says red light, all the other players stop (freeze in their position). If a nearby traffic cop (adults supervising or other players) catches them moving during a red light, they receive a fine and must return to the beginning. When the traffic light says yellow players may move forward in slow motion. The first person to pass through the light becomes the new traffic light. This is a great active game to play with friends and neighbors.

 FIND OUT! When packing for your trip, what kinds of things need to be packed? Make a list for your suitcase, consult with your parents to be sure that your list is complete. Amend it if necessary, discussing why we pack certain things and leave others behind. Check off each item as you put it into your suitcase. Then, pack the list and use it to make sure you bring home everything you took, and on the back you can add all the new things they are taking home that you got on the trip.

 CHECK IT OUT! Estimate the cost of owning a car for one year. (This is especially practical for young adults who are thinking of buying a vehicle). Take a trip to a car dealership, and choose a car. Figure out what it will cost per month in payment and interest. Contact an insurance company to find out the rate for that vehicle for one year. Where will you go in this vehicle, estimate mileage, and your total cost of gas. Don't forget parking fees where applicable. Call your Secretary of State office or Department of Motor Vehicles to find out what it will cost to register your vehicle with the state. Complete the assignment by determining the number of work hours that will be required to cover the cost of ownership of this vehicle.

 TRY IT! Supplement this activity by comparing an additional vehicle or two. Determine the overall costs and decide which vehicle will be the most economical.

TRY IT! Compare the cost of vehicle ownership with other transportation options, such as public transit, carpooling, bicycling or walking.

TRY IT! Compare the total cost of purchasing a car with financing versus the cost of purchasing a vehicle with cash. Sometimes, you can negotiate a better price when you have cash up front.

TRY IT! Read the owners' manual for your family car. Learn to check tire pressure, discuss its effect on gas mileage.

Obviously, Walt Disney World is your big field trip that all this studying is building up to, but you could plan several others like the fire station, the marina (if you live close to water), an airport (even a small one). These all have vehicles that you can visit and study their uses. You may even be able to talk them into letting you try out the siren.

TRY IT! Be a pilot on the monorail. Get in line to ride in the very front car with the driver. This may be a little bit complicated if there are more than four in your group, as only four may ride at a time. The rest of your group can wait for the next one, or can ride in another car.

"We never had to wait in line for this spot, even when there seemed to be a crowd otherwise."

The cast member working there will let you know if the driver is taking passengers.

"We never had anyone say no, but they were very strict about only four at a time, even the hand held baby couldn't ride with us."

The view from the front of the monorail is unlike any you will get elsewhere in the park. You can ask questions of the driver as long as you are careful not to distract him.

"We learned that in Japan, seven urban areas use monorails as their primary form of public transportation and that they even make a profit. This is quite a contrast from public transportation in most U.S. cities, which require tax funding to continue running."

At the end of the ride, you will receive a co-pilot license. It is about the size of a business card and will serve as a souvenir later.

There are many forms of transportation in the Magic Kingdom. Keep a running tally to see how many examples you can find of each. Add your ideas to this list.

Cars

Horses

Bicycles

Trains

Boats

Line Time: Take turns telling parts of a story based on these questions. If you could travel anywhere in the world, where would it be? If you could travel by any mode of transportation in the world, what would it be?

✋ TRY IT! Make models of the different types of transportation you found, using any materials that are readily available to you. Choose a method of transportation from any period in history. As you are building the model, discuss the similarities and differences between the method of transportation you've chosen to build and others. Also, discuss the differences in the cultures that used these methods of transportation. The level of difficulty can range from toddlers making a car or train out of a cardboard box to a Playdoh/clay sculpture to an elaborate balsa wood structure made without written instructions by a high school student.

✋ TRY IT & FIND OUT! Make a boat model that will really float. To see how far your boat will travel, put a small note with your phone number or a mailing address (or 📖 email). (Get your parents permission first) into a Ziploc bag and attach it to the 🐿 inside of your boat. The note should indicate the purpose of your experiment, and let people know that you would like them to put the boat back into the water (with the note) and to contact you to let you know where they saw it.
☑ CHECK IT OUT! Read the book, "Paddle to the Sea." to learn about the results of a similar experiment.

✋ TRY IT! Make a scrapbook page or mural that's all about vehicles. Get your picture taken on every type of transportation you encounter: here are some ideas: At the train station, pose with the conductor. Stand in front of the monorail, and hold up your pilot's license. Visit the fire station and police station; ask if you can pose from the driver's seat. Pose for a shot from the seat of a rocket on Space Mountain. How many more ideas can you think of? Write a list here and check them off as you collect them. Have fun!

Souvenir Idea: If you rode the monorail and received a co-pilots license, you can add an appropriate sized picture of yourself and laminate the two together. Ask your parents to show you their drivers' license or other form of identification. Learn what they are used for.

TRY IT! Make a transportation mural. Find the different methods of transportation in a magazine and cut them out. Glue these onto a piece of posterboard.

 TRY IT! Graphing activity. Organize pictures of transportation into groups: Example: four wheels, two wheels, or no wheels. Example: Land transport, Sea transport, or Air transport. Make a graph of the different types of transportation that you used throughout your vacation.

 TRY IT! Make a vehicle book. This could be a great way to display the photos you took in the last activity. Choose a vehicle type, and draw an outline of it. Cut out one for a stencil, trace it onto several pieces of construction paper, and cut them all out. Stack these up and choose an edge to use for the binding (this is usually the top or the left side). Stitch the edge together with needle and thread. Now, you have a transportation book. Draw pictures or insert photographs, add stickers, tell stories of the adventures you've had finding all kinds of vehicles.
Pre writers can dictate their stories for mom and dad to write in.

 TRY IT! Make some vehicle shaped sculptures. Use Playdoh or Sculpey clay. TASTE IT! Use a sugar cookie recipe to make some dough for shaping. Cookie cutters can be found at a variety of locations, or you can use your template from above and trace the flattened dough with a knife. Bake up those yummy cut outs and have some milk and cookies while you share a good book, like the one you made in the previous activity.
Here is a simple sugar cookie recipe if you don't already have one:

2 3/4 cup flour	1 cup butter, softened
1 tsp. baking soda	1 1/2 cup sugar
1/2 tsp. baking powder	1 egg
Combine dry ingredients in small bowl.	2 tsp. vanilla

Blend wet ingredients in large bowl.
Add dry ingredients. Mix well. Refrigerate for 2-4 hours before trying to shape and cut. For plain round cookies, these can be baked immediately. Roll into balls the size of a ping pong ball, and place onto cookie sheet or baking stone. Bake at 375 for 8 minutes. When you use the refrigerated dough, roll it out flat and cut into shapes. Place these onto your cookie sheet or baking stone and bake at 375 for 8 minutes. Do not overcook, instead, pull them from the oven, and leave them on the pan to cool.

Geography Fun! Studying US History would be incomplete without some geography lessons to go along with it. For this game: you will need a USA map.

This is a logic puzzle. I am going to tell you a story and your goal is to decipher the answer based on all the clues working together. My friend Lucy and I left Detroit to-gether, but we were never in the same state again until we met up at our final destination. Neither Lucy or I ever visited the same state twice. By the end of the clues, you should be able to identify every state that Lucy visited, every state that I visited, and every state that was never visited by either of us, and finally, your detective work should lead you to answer this question: Where did Lucy and I meet up at the end of our trip? You may want to have a reproducible copy of your map so you can mark off states as you eliminate them as possible an-swers.

Clue 1 There are clues in the directions.

Clue 2 I started out going northwest, all the way to the Pacific Ocean in fact. My first stop was in a state that starts with the same letter as the state that Lucy first visited. Then, I headed south just one state and almost caught up with Lucy, but ended up in the state right next to the one she was in on her second stop, which was only one state west of where she was on her first stop.

Clue 3 Neither Lucy or I has ever left the contiguous United States. I flew east to Richmond, while Lucy went south to Phoenix.

Clue 4 I flew to the biggest state and Lucy went to the smallest state. We both wanted to see the Hersey factory, but neither of us ever made it to that state.

Clue 5 Of the states that were left, I visited all the ones that start with the letter 'I' and ended up in the 'I' state farthest to the east, but neither I nor Lucy ever visited the four letter state right next to it.

Clue 6 Lucy has been to every state that begins with the letter 'm' and ended up in the 'm' state that is farthest to the south. Neither of us traveled to the state di-rectly north or the one directly east of this 'm' state.

Clue 7 Lucy and I each only visited one state each that touches the Gulf of Mex-ico, but I did visit a state with the same name as our country neighbor to the south.

Clue 8 Neither of us ever visited a state with the word north, south, east or west in the name, but Lucy made her next stop in a large eastern state with the word NEW in it. Two other states with the word New were never visited at all.

Clue 9 Our final destination was not Colorado or any state that touches it.

Clue 10 Lucy's longest flight went from Vermont to California. Her shortest flight went from Wisconsin to Arkansas. Neither of these was her final flight.

Clue 11 My longest flight went from Connecticut to Nevada. My shortest flight went from Georgia to Kentucky. Neither of these was my last flight.

The one state that has not been eliminated is the final destination of our trip. Think you have it figured out? The answer is at the end of the book.

Here's another Geography Game to play with a USA map.
Make up clues for friends and family to solve in order to find their way through the maze of states. Here are some clues for younger kids.

EXAMPLE: Find the state you live in, color it blue. Find the largest state, color it green. Find the smallest state, color it yellow. Put an x on every state you've ever visited. Color black the state(s) you will drive through (or fly over) on your way to Disney.

Come up with some more clues to go with this idea.

CHECK IT OUT! Compare the flying route to the driving route. Using a map, plot the starting and ending point of your travels. Figure out how many miles you will travel, and how long it will take to get there. For a more challenging activity, compare the cost of flying versus the cost of driving. Consider the cost of meals, gas, oil changes, and so on.

TRY IT! Another game suggestion! You will need a United States road atlas labeled with the names of the states and the capitals, and fifty index cards. Write the name of one capital city and state on each index card. Take turns pulling two cards from the deck, the first card names the location that your trip begins at, and the second card names the location that your trip ends at. Plan your route on the road map. How many miles will you have to travel? If you travel on highways, you can average 65 mph, but on state or county roads, you can only average 45mph. See who can find the shortest route? Who can find the fastest route?

Flag Folding Ceremony
Town Square

Every year, we witness Scout troops carrying the flag in our local parades. We see them participate in flag ceremonies, but through this study, we learned how much more meaningful this is than just the putting away of the flag for the night. At most locations the raising of the flag takes place at sunrise and the retreat takes place at dusk. The flag should be raised quickly, but be brought down slowly. The following ceremony is taken from the United States Air Force Academy.

The emcee begins reading as the Honor Guard is coming forward.
"The flag folding ceremony represents the same religious principles on which our country was originally founded. The portion of the flag denoting honor is the canton of blue containing the stars representing the states our veterans served in uniform. The canton field of blue dresses from left to right and is inverted when draped as a pall on a casket of a veteran who has served our country in uniform.

In the Armed Forces of the United States, at the ceremony of retreat the flag is lowered, folded in a triangle fold and kept under watch throughout the night as a tribute to our nation's honored dead. The next morning it is brought out and, at the ceremony of reveille, run aloft as a symbol of our belief in the resurrection of the body."

(Wait for the Honor Guard or Flag Detail to unravel and fold the flag into a quarter fold—resume reading when Honor Guard is standing ready.)
"The first fold of our flag is a symbol of life.

The second fold is a symbol of our belief in the eternal life.

The third fold is made in honor and remembrance of the veteran departing our ranks who gave a portion of life for the defense of our country to attain a peace throughout the world.

The fourth fold represents our weaker nature, for as American citizens trusting in God, it is to Him we turn in times of peace as well as in times of war for His divine guidance.

The fifth fold is a tribute to our country, for in the words of Stephen Decatur, "Our country, in dealing with other countries, may she always be right; but it is still our country, right or wrong."

The sixth fold is for where our hearts lie. It is with our heart that we pledge allegiance to the flag of the United States of America, and to the republic for which it stands, one nation, under God, indivisible, with liberty and justice for all.

The seventh fold is a tribute to our Armed Forces, for it is through the Armed Forces that we protect our country and our flag against all her enemies, whether they be found within or without the boundaries of our republic.

The eighth fold is a tribute to the one who entered into the valley of the shadow of death, that we might see the light of day, and to honor mother, for whom it flies on Mother's Day.

The ninth fold is a tribute to womanhood; for it has been through their faith, love, loyalty and devotion that the character of the men and women who have made this country great have been molded.

The tenth fold is a tribute to the father, for he, too, has given his sons and daughters for the defense of our country since they were first born.

The eleventh fold represents the lower portion of the seal of King David and King Solomon, and glorifies the God of Abraham, Isaac, and Jacob.

The twelfth fold represents an emblem of eternity and glorifies God the Father, the Son, and Holy Ghost.

When the flag is completely folded, the stars are uppermost, reminding us of our national motto, "In God we Trust."

(Wait for the Honor Guard or Flag Detail to inspect the flag—after the inspection, resume reading.)

After the flag is completely folded and tucked in, it takes on the appearance of a cocked hat; ever reminding us of the soldiers who served under General George Washington, and the sailors and marines who served under Captain John Paul Jones who were followed by their comrades and shipmates in the Armed Forces of the United States, preserving for us the rights, privileges, and freedoms we enjoy today."

This Flag Folding Ceremony is from the US Air Force Academy, 2001.

At the Magic Kingdom, in Town Square at dusk, you can see the flag retreat ceremony done by Disney. There is not an emcee, but the national anthem is played as they retire the flag. The Town Square is at the entrance to Main Street, USA. Typically, the flag is raised quickly in the morning and lowered slowly in the evening. The flag should be displayed daily and on all holidays at all public institutions, polling locations, and schools. When displayed on a surface, the blue field belongs in the left upper corner. When in the presence of the flag, everyone should stand with their right hand on their heart. The flag should never touch anything beneath it, or be allowed to touch the ground. When flown or carried with other flags the American flag must always be flown the highest, and never on the same pole as another flag.

The United States flag is never retreated from the following locations:

Fort McHenry in Maryland

Flaghouse Square, Maryland

U.S. Marine Corps Memorial, Virginia

The White House, Washington D.C.

U.S. Customs Port of Entry

Grounds of National Memorial Arch, Valley Forge, Pennsylvania

The Pledge of Allegiance to the American flag: "I pledge allegiance to the flag of the United States of America, to the republic for which it stands, one nation under God, indivisible, with liberty and justice for all.

As a side note, and I am deeply saddened to have to include this. At the time of this writing, Satan is attacking our men and women in uniform and demanding that this flag folding ceremony be declared unconstitutional. We pray that our fallen soldiers continue to be given the respect that they deserve and that the Truth of those words not be hidden. Please join us in that prayer.

☑ CHECK IT OUT!
There's a bench here in Town Square where Roy Disney and Minnie Mouse sit together and watch the crowds pass by.

Mickey's Toon Town Fair

In 1988, this area opened as Mickey's birthdayland as a celebration of Mickey's 60th. It is now more of a quaint countryside village in the middle of their perpetual county fair. The area is filled with striped fair tents and the homes of Mickey, Minnie, Donald and Goofy. This is the place "Where the County Fair Never Ends".

"We think this is a "HOT SPOT FOR COOL RELIEF"... that means there is plenty of opportunity for everyone in the group to get wet."

The Barnstormer at Goofy's Wiseacre Farm is the only ride in this area, good for young ones who love the thrill rides but are too short to ride Disney's BIG mountains. The story here is that you are riding in a plane (probably a crop duster) with Goofy who is such a great pilot (add sarcasm) that he flies right into the side of his barn. There is no height requirement, but it is recommended for children three and up.

Mickey's country house contains a mess in the kitchen from Donald and Goofy trying to help redecorate. Out in the back yard is a garden of Mickey shaped vegetables.

Minnie's country house contains foam furniture, and lots of surprises to find.

✋ Try out the answering machine; play the messages. What is the food cooking in the kitchen? Is there anything special in the refrigerator?

❓ Did you know Minnie is the editor of her own magazine? Minnie Cartoon Country Living.

Donald's boat is named Miss Daisy, for his true love. But, Donald has not taken very good care of her and she is often springing a leak. What a thrill for the short crew to run around trying to plug them up (Be Prepared to get Soaked!)

If you would like to meet and greet the characters; look for Mickey in the judges' tent behind his house, find Minnie in her garden, Donald and Goofy are behind the Toon Town Hall of Fame. The Hall of Fame has three sections; Classic, Winnie the Pooh, and the villains. There are usually three characters inside each section.

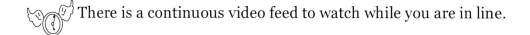 There is a continuous video feed to watch while you are in line.

Step into more recent history at MGM Studios. The whole place is designed to feel like a walk through old time Hollywood. Plan to eat at the Prime Time Café, which at first glance might seem like a 1950's diner, but it is something else entirely. You will enter a typical 1950's home, where if you happen to get seated right away, spend some time after you eat exploring the lobby (living room). Mom is in the kitchen cooking up some grub and cousin Lorraine is your babysitter...

"The staff here is required to do a lot of improvisation. The story line gets better and better as the meal goes on. Don't plan on this being a quick meal."

Whether you are the youngest, the oldest or even the parent in your own home, here you are all kids, and you better behave. The rules for the dining room are clearly set forth, and mischievous children should expect to be reprimanded. This is a good time to discuss changes in ideas about discipline and their affects on our society. For this generations children, there is a television in every dining room airing clips from old shows like I Love Lucy, Dennis the Menace and Donna Reed.

Tomorrow Land
Map

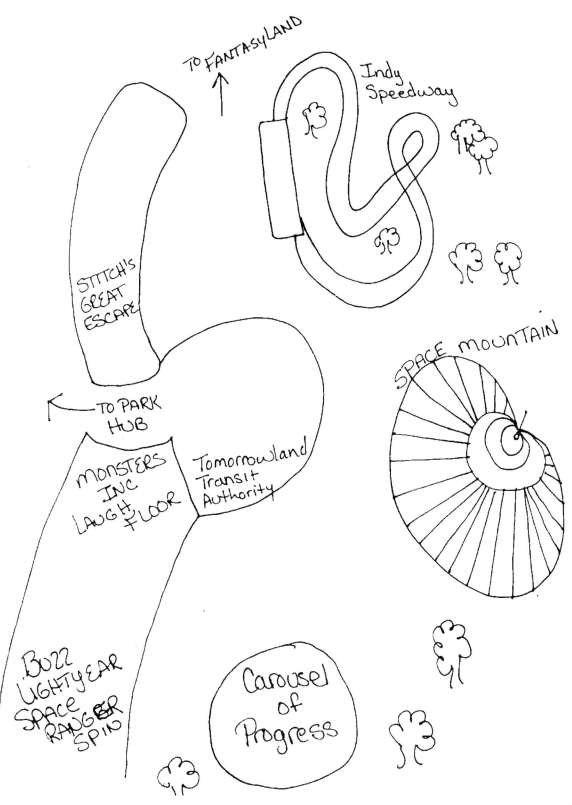

TO FANTASYLAND

Indy Speedway

STITCH'S GREAT ESCAPE

SPACE MOUNTAIN

TO PARK HUB

MONSTERS INC LAUGH FLOOR

Tomorrowland Transit Authority

BUZZ LIGHTYEAR SPACE RANGER SPIN

Carousel of Progress

Tomorrowland

The first vision of Tomorrow was a scene set in 1986; we've come a long way from that. The other lands are nostalgic and the attractions we remember from our childhood are still very much the same. In such cases, we would like them to never change, but to be just as magical for our children as they were for us in our childhood. Tomorrowland, in contrast, is by design an ever changing element. If it doesn't continue to change and evolve with the times, then it ceases to be a representation of tomorrow and is instead a glimpse of yesterday.

Tomorrowland was initially designed as a futuristic view of our culture, but EPCOT replaced that idea and by the 1990's, 1986 was no longer a vision of the future. This area is constantly being updated. It had a major redo in 1995 featuring rockets and aliens, and so became a vision of the future through the eyes of children.

TRY IT! See a Tomorrowland phone, pick it up and see who answers.

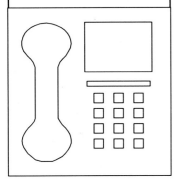

 TRY IT! Make a list of items that could help you or someone you know, but that hasn't been invented yet. Think about the processes you've learned about and write an essay about how one of these items might be invented in the future.

✓ CHECK IT OUT! Make a list of ten things that didn't exist when you were born.

 FIND OUT! Pick one item from the list and learn about how it was invented.

 TRY IT! Create a design for what you think it will look like in the future.
What kinds of advances do you think will be made in its technology over the next twenty years?
What would you improve?

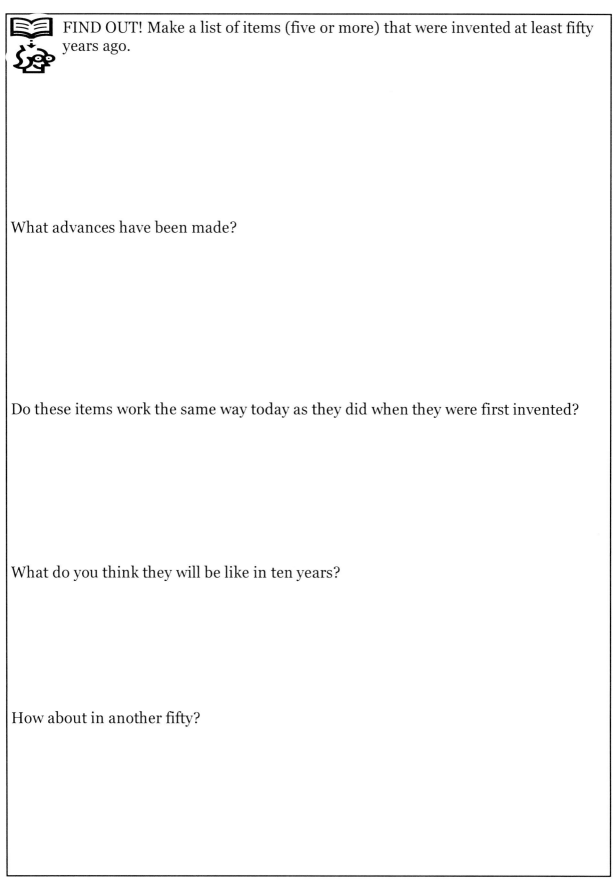

FIND OUT! Make a list of items (five or more) that were invented at least fifty years ago.

What advances have been made?

Do these items work the same way today as they did when they were first invented?

What do you think they will be like in ten years?

How about in another fifty?

Blueline Express

This ride will take you slowly and gently through Space Mountain, where you can get a glimpse of the track and the cars. It is also known as the Tomorrowland Transit Authority or TTA.

This could be the new wave in public transportation if it wasn't so slow. It works on linear induction motors. Electro magnets pull the train along the track. It requires very little power usage and produces no pollution. Could it be the public transportation of tomorrow?

 FIND OUT! What options do people have for public transportation?

Analyze each of these options.
Which are the fastest?

Which are the most convenient for citizens?

Which are the best for the environment?

Which are the best for the future of the communities that they are in?

Compare the pros and cons of each type of public transit.

 TRY IT! Be a city planner! What would you recommend for your community as a plan for public transportation that will lead your town into the future?

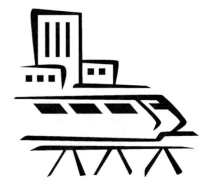

Stitch's Great Escape

Because the theming of Tomorrowland is all about the future, it has to be ever changing. Otherwise, the present catches up to the idea of the future and then it becomes the past, allowing for a new future to take its place. This space has been

Flight to the Moon (1971 to 1975)

Mission to Mars (1975 to 1993)

The ExtraTERRORestrial Alien Encounter (1995 to 2003)

Stitch's Great Escape (2004 to present) This attraction is very similar to Alien Encounter, but much sillier, which I suppose allows it to be less frightening.

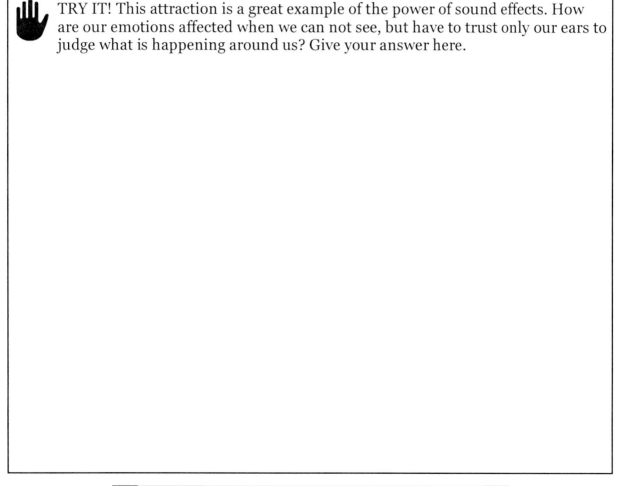

TRY IT! This attraction is a great example of the power of sound effects. How are our emotions affected when we can not see, but have to trust only our ears to judge what is happening around us? Give your answer here.

LINK TO MGM! Drew Carey Sounds Dangerous!

Monsters, Inc Laugh Floor

 DID YOU KNOW? This location used to house the TimeKeeper.

 CHECK IT OUT! It requires lots of audience participation, and provides plenty of corny jokes.

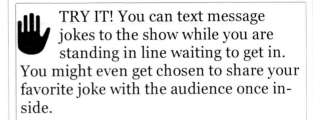 TRY IT! You can text message jokes to the show while you are standing in line waiting to get in. You might even get chosen to share your favorite joke with the audience once inside.

Could this be the future of animation? You've studied film and animation, theater and live entertainment, learned about Walt and his animated creations, so tell us what you think!

What everyone really wants to know is...

"How do they animate that fast?"

Can you find the answer?

 FIND OUT! In this attraction, it appears as though the animated characters on the screen are interacting with audience members, responding to their comments, and answering their questions.

How does this work?

When you find out, send us a letter, we'd like to know.

 CHECK IT OUT! If you really like this show, you'll appreciate Turtle Talk with Crush over at the Living Seas Pavilion in Epcot Center.

Indy Speedway

Men are competitive by design. So, before there were cars, they were racing everything else, horses, camels, donkeys or whatever. The ancient Greeks were racing on foot.

The first organized auto races began in 1894 to test durability, stamina, and performance of the vehicles. Many manufacturers brought cars in to compete with each other.

By the 1930's, open road racing had been banned (for safety reasons) in most places and manufacturers were designing cars specifically for racing, no longer using their domestic automobiles for this purpose. Automobile racing is now one of the top five spectator sporting events.

 FIND OUT! More about the history of this and other types of racing.

Carl Graham Fisher was one of the first in the auto industry to suggest an "automotive proving grounds" (these are studied in more detail in the chapter on Test Trak in Vacation Education destination Epcot). The technology in auto manufacturing outpaced the development of reliable roadways, making it difficult to guage the maximum performance capabilities of a vehicle. He designed the track that is now home to the Indy 500, a place where cars could be pushed to their limits, just so men could see what those limits are.

 DID YOU KNOW? The first 500 race was won by a car whose top speed was less than 75 mph.

 FIND OUT! What is the current record for the top speed of a car winning the Indy 500 in modern times?

"The line out in front of this attraction to get a photo opportunity with the race car was almost as long as the line to ride the actual attraction. I don't know which was more exciting."

"The cars in this raceway travel at a whopping seven miles an hour, which by the way feels really fast when your seven year old slams on the brakes and the seat belt pushes the food that was in your stomach to... well to somewhere else."

CHECK IT OUT! This is a website that will give you a good start in your research. http://www.autoracinghistory.com

Space Mountain
Roller Coaster: You must be 44inches tall to ride

Vocabulary

Roller Coaster

Designers

Isaac Newton

Newton's laws

Friction

Potential energy

Kinetic energy

La Marcus Adna Thompson

Space Mountain opened in December 1974, and is one of only two true roller coasters in Magic Kingdom. It took ten years for Walt's idea of a ride through outer space to be developed, and two more years to get it built.

This ride travels through the dark reaching top speeds of 28 mph. In comparison, the first coaster to open at Cedar Point (known as the worlds greatest roller coast) had a frightening first hill that stood 25 feet tall and it traveled at 10 mph. That was pretty scary in 1892. Today, the worlds fastest roller coaster is Kingda Ka in New Jersey, reaching speeds of up to 128 mph. Space Mountain does feel faster than it is because of the dark, but as a roller coaster, it does come in at the slow end. It's steepest drop is 39 degrees; the current record is held at 97 degrees. To put this into perspective, a straight drop is 90 degrees.

 FIND OUT! Study the advances in coaster technology and the designers who made them happen.

"We were able to trace coaster beginnings all the way to the 14th century ."

BABY TIP! The Tomorrowland Light and Power Co. is where Space Mountain exits. There is a shopping area and a video arcade. This is a fun place for kids to play while they wait for riders.

☑ CHECK IT OUT! Research the history and creation of roller coasters and other amusement rides.

La Marcus Adna Thompson is credited with the patent for the first roller coaster in January of 1885. The hands and minds of many inventors, scientists, engineers and enthusiasts have worked on improving this thrill ride ever since.

It takes a build up of potential energy (like when the train is pulled or pushed up the first hill). This is converted to kinetic energy (like the force of gravity pulling the train down the hill). It converts back to potential energy as the train rises up the second smaller hill. Gradually, energy is lost due to the force of friction, forcing each subsequent hill to be smaller.

✋ TRY IT! Build a timeline based on your research of roller coasters.

📖 FIND OUT! The definition of a roller coaster. Write your answer here.

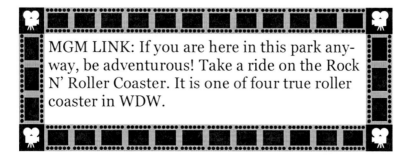

MGM LINK: If you are here in this park anyway, be adventurous! Take a ride on the Rock N' Roller Coaster. It is one of four true roller coaster in WDW.

CHECK IT OUT! Newton's Third Law states, "for every action, there is an equal and opposite reaction". Consider this when you are swimming. Place your hand in the water and push. Can you feel the pressure of the water pushing back against your hand? This is an example of Newton's Third Law. The pressure you feel is equal in force to your push, but it is opposite in direction as the water pushes against your hand. Fish are able to swim by taking advantage of this; their fins push the water in one direction and the water pushes back on the fish, propelling it through the water. Birds are able to fly because their wings push down on the air and the air pushes back up on the bird. What an Amazing Creation!

As you fly up and down the hills, around the curves, upside down and inside out of roller coasters, consider that you are relying on the laws of physics to get you safely back to where you started from. There is no engine system to pull or push you through the ride. The train is pulled to the top of the first hill, and then gravity takes over and the cars must complete the track with their existing energy. This is similar to sledding. If you live in a northern climate, you've probably been snow sledding. You drag the sled to the top of the hill (your energy), and then you sit and ride it to the bottom (your energy converted). The higher and steeper the hill, the harder (more energy) it is to carry the sled up, but the faster and more thrilling the ride. If you've never been around snow, you've probably tried this with a wagon or go cart or even on your bicycle. Pedal to the top of a hill and then put your feet up while you fly back down. The amount of energy you put into getting to the top of the hill (potential energy) is directly proportionate to the speed and energy (kinetic energy or energy of motion) used to get you to the bottom.

This is exactly what some people in Russia were thinking in the 1600's. They formed huge blocks of ice into sleds, stuffing straw into a chiseled hole to make a comfortable seat. How did they stop them? No brakes, but they did have the forethought to throw down sand in front of them. Now, go study friction!

TRY IT! & FIND OUT! Go to the closest playground with a big slide in jeans. Take a matchbox car and a stopwatch along for your experiment. Send the car down the slide, and time it. Send yourself down the slide and time your descent. You may need a partner to work the stop watch while you are sliding. Which is faster? You or the car? Why? You weigh more and so the force of gravity is greater on you. It takes more energy to get you to the top of the ladder than the car. Should you go down faster than the car? If you are wearing jeans, the car was probably much faster than you. FIND OUT WHY!

CHECK IT OUT! Explore a Career! Research what it takes to become an engineer who designs and builds roller coasters and other types of rides. Check out a website run by roller coaster fans such as ACE (American Coaster Enthusiasts) who are the current and up and coming designers for new rides? What do the fans want from them? What qualifications are needed for this type of job?

In the early 1800's, the French developed wooden sleds with iron runners, and sent them down tracks made of rollers (thus the term coasting the rollers or roller coasting). In 1817, they figured out how to make a cart go fast enough to complete a u-turn in the track and make its way back to the start.

The coaster commonly called "America's first" was a gravity switchback train designed by La Marcus Adna Thompson and built at Coney Island. This involved starting at a height and using gravity to send you down the first hill, then when the sled stopped, the riders would get off. Workers would push or drag the sled onto a new height and riders would re-board, and ride back to the starting point. It cost five cents to ride and they made over $600 a day when it opened. The cost to build it was recouped in just a few short weeks, and their success encouraged inventors who rushed to improve upon its design. Almost immediately, Phillip Hinckle invented a steam powered chain lift to tug coasters to new heights and increase the potential down hill speed.

Most people were familiar with the parks at Coney Island and similar locations, as these were very popular. The rail road companies kept their trains full with commuters all throughout the week, but ran empty on the weekends. So, they developed parks at the end of the rail line to attract customers to ride on the weekend away from the city out to a rural retreat. But, even before this, people were paying for the thrill of a coaster.

America's real first coaster, was not a coaster at all, but the Mauch Chunk railway. The train was made to haul coal up and down the mountains of Pennsylvania. When the mine shut down, the railway continued to make money by charging five cents a ride for a trip down the mountain. Mules were used to pull the train back up.

In 1846, the Centrifugal Railway in Paris opened and people tried out the upside down roller coaster. In 1895, Lina Beecher followed with the Flip Flap. However, the force required to get the cars and passengers through the loop was so great that it caused injuries. This concept did not make a comeback until the 1970's.

After the stock market crash of 1929, and then the onset of WWII, roller coaster technological advances slowed down, as did most industries in the United States that weren't war related.

In 1953, Walt Disney asked Ed Morgan and Karl Bacon of Arrow Development to design some rides for the theme park he had planned. In 1955, Disneyland opened in California, and over the next several years, Arrow would be responsible for such rides as Tea Cups, Carousel, Snow White's Adventures, Dumbo, It's a Small World, Pirates of the Carribean, and the Haunted Mansion. They also developed rides for other amusement parks such as the log flume ride and it was Arrow who in the 70's was responsible for the comeback of loop-de-loops.

Arrow produced the Matterhorn that Disney introduced in 1959, the first tubular steel coaster. Steel rides were quieter and smoother as the pieces were welded together, eliminating the clickety clack of running over the joints of a wooden coaster. More importantly though, steel could be bent and twisted in ways that wood never could. Many of the features we take for granted in roller coasters today come from that initial concept.

Some kids will gleefully board every ride, and are offended when told they might not be "big" enough. I have one of those kids. Some kids won't ride anything no matter what. I have one of those. If you have kids who don't like to ride roller coasters, or they do and you don't, there is no need to worry. There are only four roller coasters in all of Walt Disney World.

FIND OUT! Can you figure out which four rides qualify as true roller coasters? Hint: Two of them are in Magic Kingdom.

Then, there are the kids who may or may not be convinced to ride, but need answers to several questions before they even get near it. I also have one of those. Here are a few things those personality types like to know.

1. Could the train come off the track? Not likely. Coasters are designed with three kinds of wheels. The running wheels are the main wheels that run down the track, like wagon wheels down the sidewalk. A second set of wheels called friction wheels keep the car from going from side to side. The last set are probably the most important, and they are commonly called upstop wheels. These are under the track, and yet still connected to the car, and they make it possible for the train to stay on the track even if you go upside down. You might at first think that you wouldn't need these unless you were going upside down, but the force that lifts you up and out of your seat at times would also send the train up and off the track if not for these. If you were to look under the track, you might see a solid metal bar instead of wheels, but it does the same job.

TRY IT! Take a wagon to the top of a hill, and let it go. Try to make sure there is nothing in the way that might get damaged. If you don't have a wagon, a toy dump truck or something similar will work as well. The point is to send it down the hill and see if it goes straight. It will probably go from side to side, possibly leaving the ground at points depending on the grade of the hill and it might even tip over. This is essentially how those first rides down the icy slopes in Russia went, and how your ride would likely go without those wheels.

2. How come gravity doesn't pull the train back down the first (lift) hill? Good question. It actually would if the chain that was pulling it up the hill stopped working. But, a mechanism referred to as 'dogs' stops that from happening by acting like a set of stairs, that the train sits on. Each click you hear going up the lift hill is the train moving up onto the next step, so if the chain broke, you would not fall backwards, but you would just sit there until someone came to let you out.

TRY IT! Take a small box and tie a piece of rope around it. Set the box at the bottom of a set of stairs. Now, you go stand a few steps up, or even at the very top if your rope is long enough. From the top step, pull on the rope until the box is above the first step. You should be able to let the rope hang loose and the box will fall to the first step, but not back down to the landing where it started. Even if you let go of the rope completely, the box would still just sit there on the last step that you had pulled it to. You can do this again and again at each step until you reach the top, to illustrate how a roller coaster reaches the top of the lift hill.

3. What makes it go so fast? It really isn't going much faster than you did in your car on the way to Orlando. Space Mountain's top speed is less than thirty miles per hour, but you may feel you are going much faster because you can not see. Big Thunder Mountain also reaches top speeds of about thirty miles per hour, but the thrills come from the theming, not from the speed. When you are focused on the scenery or in the case of Space Mountain, you can't see the tracks, then the twists and turns take you by surprise.

TRY IT! This is best done outdoors. Create a path way for a race. It should go up and down grades and have lots of turns. Make it as long as you can. Fill a glass full (all the way to the top) with water, and go through the path as fast as you can without spilling any of the water. With only one child, use a stopwatch and try to beat your own best time. If you run the course, you will likely have very little water left in the glass. If possible, try this same experiment while being pulled in a wagon or sled down the same track. The forces (remember Newton's laws of physics that you looked up?) at work on your body when riding a roller coaster are similar to the forces at work on the glass as you run with it through the obstacle course.

4. Will I fall out? Not if you wear your seat belt. Rock N' Roller Coaster is the only one in WDW that goes upside down, and centripetal force will keep you in your seat. Want to know what centripetal force is? Centripetal force is a term in your vocabulary list... you know what to do with those don't you?

5. Why do I have to be a certain height to ride? On rides like the putt-putt type cars, the restrictions have to do with being able to reach pedals and still see over the steering wheel sufficiently. Also, the manufacturer or designer of the ride makes height recommendations based on tests that they do.

TRY IT! AT EPCOT! Ride Test Trak (if you are tall enough) and see how auto makers test automobiles for safety. The same idea is used for testing attractions. They are run with test dummies before being used by people, and also, each ride is run empty before the park opens in the morning just to be sure. Then, the maintenance folks take it for a ride to see if anything seems off. When you are at the park and a ride is closed down temporarily, it's most likely because they are making sure that everything is safe before letting you on.

6. Is it really safe? Well, probably since they would like you to go home and tell all your friends about it, and they want you to return because you loved it so much, besides, their image can't afford an accident. Injuries on rides are very rare, and the ones that do happen are usually the result of a rider who didn't follow all the posted rules, like keeping your seatbelt on and your hands and feet inside the vehicle at all times. If you want actual ride statistics, they are available from the U.S. Consumer Product Safety Commission.

This is a great lead in to learning how your states government works. The federal commission serves as an overseer of state commissions. The information you receive will include the address, phone number and likely a web site and email for your state office. You can research how your state determines the guidelines and even visit the office in your state as a field trip. Be sure to prepare interview questions for the staff, and to call in advance to make arrangements for your group.

FIND OUT! Want to know more about how coasters work? NASA created a webquest for students in grades 5-8 which challenges you to use the internet to find the answers to a series of questions. You can participate in this activity by visiting http://media.nasaexplores.com/lessons

FIND OUT!
What coaster holds the world record for speed?

For length?

For height?

What is the oldest working roller coaster in the United States?

Answers: Did you figure out which attractions are true roller coasters yet? The four true roller coasters, by definition are Space Mountain(MK), Big Thunder Mountain Railroad (MK), and Rockin' Roller Coaster(MGM), and Expedition Everest (AK). In terms of big, bad coasters, all of these guys are pretty tame. I think Splash Mountain (MK), Tower or Terror(MGM) and Test Trak (EPCOT) would qualify also, but they don't fit the definition. Now, it's time for you to ride and decide.

SPACE EXPLORATION

Vocabulary

Quasars

Pulsars

Novas

Supernovas

Black hole

Dwarf star

Giant star

Variable star

Cosmic cloud

Globular cluster

Asteroids

Comet

telescope

TRY IT! Develop a scale model of our solar system. Answer this: Is it possible to create a model of the sun and earth to scale? What would you have to use? If the earth is one centimeter in diameter, how large would the sun have to be?

FIND OUT! Learn the names of the planets in order from the sun. You can use an acronym such as "My Very Energetic Mother Just Served Us Nine Pizzas". If you can remember this sentence you can remember the first letter of each of the planets, Mercury, Venus, Earth, Mars, Jupiter, Saturn, Uranus, Neptune, and Pluto. Another one I like is "Many Voices Enjoy Making Jungle Sounds Under Nana's Porch." If you don't like either of these, you can make up your own. It doesn't matter how ridiculous the sentence is if you'll remember it, then you have a better chance of remembering the planets names also.

Note: There is some disagreement among scientists as to whether or not Pluto is still a planet. If you prefer, here are alternate acronyms: "My Very Energetic Mother Just Served Us Nachos" or "Many Voices Enjoy Making Jungle Noises Until Nighttime"

CHECK IT OUT! Explore a career in Space Exploration. What is required of an astronaut? Do all astronauts get to go into space? How much and what kind of education do you need to work for NASA? Make a list of the positive and negative aspects of the job. How about being an engineer? The designer of a space craft?

TRY IT! Theoretically, it might be possible for humans to one day live in space. Although, it would seem from all current knowledge that God has already given us one planet perfectly designed as a habitat, it is unlikely that we will discover another. There is however a chance that we could create an artificial atmosphere that would sustain life. If this were possible, design a poster or write an essay to show what life might be like in this new community.

TRY IT! Using materials that are readily accessible to you, design and build a vehicle that could travel into space.

 FIND OUT! Discover how space travel vehicles work.

 How are they designed and built?

How would you improve upon existing designs?

 CHECK IT OUT! Read past issues of newspapers and magazines to find out what kind of problems NASA has had in the past with space travel.

 TRY IT! Come up with suggestions to help solve some of these problems?

TRY IT! Use this space to tell a story using as many of your vocabulary words as possible. Use additional paper if needed.

Buzz Lightyear's Space Ranger Spin

This space has changed over the years.

If you had wings (1972 to 1987)

If you could fly (1987 to 1989)

Delta Dream Flight (1989 to 1995)

Take Flight (1996 to 1998)

Buzz has been flying around this space since 1998. This is a family favorite, everyone can ride, everyone can participate. The storyline is that Buzz needs help to defeat Zurg, and so you are invited to assist in this task. In the end, you are successful. But the real reason families get back on this ride over and over again is the competitive sport of it. Two guests ride per car and shoot at targets. Each target has a point value, the harder it is to hit, the more points it's worth. Your score is tabulated and displayed on a screen on the front of your ride car. When the ride is over, compare scores with the other members of your group. The low scorers will be begging for a shot to redeem themselves.

This is a great example of the future of family game night. Our game nights currently consist of an occasional board game, but more often than not, we play some form of competitive video arcade system game.

I grew up playing board games like Monopoly, Clue and Life. My mother played Card Games like Rummy, and Pinochle. My grandmothers generation played games like cribbage. What about your family? How has family game night changed for you? Do you play the same games you remember from your childhood? Are these the same games your parents played as children?

 FIND OUT! Ask members of your family, from several generations to name as many of the games from their childhood that they can remember playing as a family. How many of those games are still in your home today?
What makes a good family game?

 TRY IT! Pass on the traditions of the games that you played when you were young. Hold a family game night! Learn the rules for some new games and some

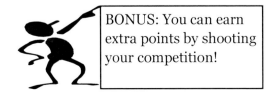 BONUS: You can earn extra points by shooting your competition!

Carousel of Progress

This attraction was first shown at the 1964-65 World's Fair. The theme song was written by Richard and Robert Sherman. It has six theaters, 240 seats in each one. The seats rotate around the stage, which showcases the development of progress by looking into the homes of the average family over the past century.

This is one of the few attractions still in existence at the WDW parks that was hand selected by Walt himself. Be sure to see it. As you view the ever changing stage, think about how you would answer these questions:

In each scene, how is the news delivered?

In each scene, what things are the children of that generation involved in?

In each scene, what new gadgets are being introduced to make life more convenient?

Write down a few questions of your own to look for as the scenery changes through each decade, what are the "signs of the times" for that generation?

Traveling Games
And Other Stuff

This is not a unit study in itself, but I wanted to include a few games and activities that you can do on the way, and some extra stuff that ties into your vacation as a whole.

☑ CHECK IT OUT! If you happen to have a Sega Dreamcast (Does that make us really old?) There's a fun video game called Disney's Magical Racing Tour where you can take turns driving through many of the popular attractions, including the Haunted Mansion and Space Mountain.

✋ TRY IT! Play the alphabet game. Working your way from a to z, or from z to a, find each letter of the alphabet in order. You must find each letter you are looking for before finding the next. For instance if you are looking for a G, but see an S, the S does not count. You must see the letters in order. You should establish rules in advance about where they can be, like on billboards, road signs, semi trailers, license plates, etc.

"We usually rule that it can be on anything as long as it is outside the vehicle.

Now, tie it into your studies. This time work your way from a to z, or from z to a, naming a person, place or event in US history following the same rules as before.

✋ TRY IT! Designate one person in your group to be the Timekeeper. This is a great activity for a child who has just recently learned to tell time. Have them determine the actual wait time for each attraction and compare this with the estimated wait time posted at the entrance. This person can also be in charge of making sure that the family is not late for priority seating, fast passes or other reservations. Active children will appreciate having a stop watch to play with and a task to complete during times that might otherwise be boring or frustrating.

☑ CHECK IT OUT! From you library. Stretch your mind beyond what you've learned here. When you have finished your unit studies, choose a book to read that will teach you more about one of the subjects. Then, select one or more of the following activities to complete.

1. Re-enact a scene from the book for family and friends.

2. Write a book review, and try to get it published in a newspaper or magazine.

3. Read the book aloud onto a tape and give it as a gift to someone who is unable to read. You can donate it to a children's center or a nursing home if you don't have anyone specific in mind.

TRY IT! Twenty questions, similar to I Spy. The person who is It thinks of a character, attraction or entertainer that you saw or are planning to see on your vacation. Everyone else takes turns asking questions that can be answered with a 'yes' or 'no'. If someone gets a yes answer, they can continue asking until they get a no, then it is the next person's turn, or you can just alternate turns. According to the name of the game, when twenty questions have been asked and the item has not been discovered, the 'it' person must reveal the item and gets to choose another player to think of the next item.

Example: (with four people playing)

Summer: Is it a ride? NO

Caitlin: Is it a character? YES

Caitlin: Is it a girl? NO

Tyler: Is it a boy? YES

Tyler: Did we see him in the Magic Kingdom? YES

Tyler: Did we see him on Main Street? NO

Summer: What color are his clothes? THAT'S NOT A YES OR NO QUESTION, TRY AGAIN.

Summer: Are his clothes purple? NO

Caitlin: Did we see him in ToonTown? YES

Caitlin: Is it Donald Duck? NO

Tyler: Are any of his clothes red? YES

Tyler: Is it Mickey Mouse? YES

Now, it would be Tyler's turn to be "I". He will have to think of something or someone that he saw at Walt Disney World, and the guessing will begin again. This is an excellent memory and logic game as they have to mentally sort through everything that they saw and listen carefully to the other players questions in order to eliminate enough choices that they come up with the correct answer. This game also helps to keep their memories fresh in their mind.

SOUVENIR TIP: The gift shops at the front of Magic Kingdom sell a set of postcards featuring all of the princess characters, not animated versions, but photographs of the actual cast members playing them. For less than $10 you can send all the postcards from the booklet and be left with a wallet sized photo of each for your own scrapbook. There are not a lot of bargains in Disney, but we though this one was worthwhile, as we still enjoy looking at the pictures.

SOUVENIR TIP: We found that the book prices in the park were comparable to retail elsewhere, and would recommend looking for books you like that will complement your studies while you are here. You may be able to find some of the titles used or at a discount store after you get home, but if you have a souvenir budget, this is a great way to spend it.

GO ON TOUR: Tours are an exceptional way to add to your educational experience. They range from come anytime, no charge, short tours, to make you reservations a year in advance, pay $200 per person plus your admission, all day behind the scenes tours. You can check out wdwtours online or contact them at 1-407-WDWTOUR. These informative tours can be Magic Spoilers, require a lot of walking, and may not include meals or frequent bathroom breaks. For these reasons some of the tours have a minimum age requirement. They also have several specifically for the age 3 and up crowd. Contact Disney in advance to be sure you know all the details of your tour and that it is the right one for your family.

Scavenger Hunt Ideas

In the car, on the way: Try to find the McDonalds arches. How many can you see from the highway? Try to find one for every twenty miles you travel. So, if you are driving 2000 miles; I challenge you to find those golden arches 100 times.

In the car, on the way. Have you ever played the alphabet games? Where you try to find each letter of the alphabet on a sign or license plate. Try playing this version: Find each letter of the alphabet in order, except instead of finding the actual letter, find an item that begins with the letter. Here's one possible list:

"...automobile, big rig, car, Dodge, Exxon station, Ford, Georgia license plate, Honda, ice cream shop, Jaguar, Knights Inn, Lincoln Town Car, Motorola phone, Navy bumper sticker, Odyssey by Honda, Pizza Hut, Quaker Oil, Real Estate Agent, Shell Station, Tire, Underwear (on a clothesline), vacation planner, water, extra traffic (we all agreed to count this for x), yogurt, zipper."

You can compete by writing down your answers and announcing when you are done, or work cooperatively and just shout out the answers as you see them.

Try to find the items on this list at the airport: Book store, news stand, two or more people wearing matching clothes, clocks telling the time in other time zones, map of a foreign country, find these numbers in this order 9, 8, 7, 6, 5, 4, 3, 2, 1, someone talking on a cellular phone, someone working on a laptop, a cup of coffee, someone wearing red and reading, someone sleeping, a police or security uniform, a polka-dotted tie, a double stroller, a vending machine, a pair of glasses, a piece of clothing in the color peach, a pink purse, a fluorescent yellow vest, a wheelchair, an infant safety seat, a baseball cap, a back pack that is more than one color, a cowboy hat, a Mickey Mouse shirt, a payphone, fingerprints on glass, a pilots uniform, someone with a flashlight, a ship selling hamburgers, a bird, someone running to catch their flight, an elevator, an escalator, someone listening to music, someone in a uniform not associated with the airport.

All Park Hunt: find six different kinds of transportation at each park you visit. Try to find two of each kind, land, sea, air, and try not to repeat any from one park to the next. If you visit all four parks, you should end up with twenty four different ways to travel. Moms and dad, don't be too critical, but give kids a chance to logically reason methods of travel. Like magic carpets, hang gliders, trains, rocket ships, monorails, etc.

All Parks list: These are items you can see just about anywhere on Disney property. One of the first things you should do when you arrive is pick up a park guide map. You do not need to make the hunt the focus of your visit. But, instead, read through the list of items and check, them off as you run across them. Most of them are things you will see as you tour the parks. The purpose here is to give younger children something to focus on during times when they are bored; like standing in line, or when giving another family member a chance to choose the activity.

Skink, fly, mosquito, spider, night crawler, slugs, green light, evergreen tree, orange tree, caution sign, no smoking sign, Pal Mickey, a boat you can see when you are in a boat, palm tree, American flag, candy from Goofy Candy Co., Grumpy Dwarf, photo album, helicopter, pirate ship, duck, rabbit, snail, caterpillar, Braille map, a pair of do not enter signs, the word Florida, the abbreviation FL, seashells, a Pooh bear, a tree house that did not belong to the Swiss Family Robinson, flowered skirt, hot air balloon, boarded up windows, a news stand, survey markers, Disney mail boxes, skeleton keys, refreshment station, people feeding birds, birds eating food that someone dropped, turkey leg, lasso, six-gun shooter, the sound of someone snoring, the sound of a bird chirping, a Cinderella dress on someone other than Cinderella, palm trees, red light, film projector, travel agency, a structure that looks like a building but isn't, Mr. Potato Head, a mouse award, Mickey ears, Mickey Mouse backpack, a rocket, a lasso, a lollipop shaped like Mickey, covered wagon, Mickey Mouse phone, globe, sword.

"We bought the deck of activity cards, and pulled them out every time we had to stand in line. The kids loved them. It really did make time fly."

Games To Play When Standing In Line. Here are some additional suggestions for activities to keep everyone entertained during those long waits.
Rock, Paper, Scissors
I Spy
Twenty Questions
Thumb Wrestling

Here are a few fun things that you can look for specifically in the Magic Kingdom.

Tinker Bell lives in her shop in Fantasyland. Look through the key holes in the bureau drawers and see if you can find her.

At Mickey's Philharmagic, Minnie Mouse is a founding member of this theater, can you find the large donation that she made to the theater?

Walking through Fantasyland can you see where the skyway ride used to be?

Bibliography

This is not a complete list of every resource that we used, but sometimes we found information repeated and so here we are listing the ones that we felt had the most useful information and that we would recommend you check into for additional study.

Imagineering Field Guide to Magic Kingdom at Walt Disney World, Alex Wright, Disney Enterprises 2005

The Complete Walt Disney World, Julie and Mike Neal Coconut Press, Media Enterprises, Inc.

Birnbaum's Walt Disney World for Kids by Kids, 2006 Disney Editions

Website: www.lewiscarroll.org

Website: allears.net Deb Wills

Website: www.filmsite.org

Book: Fascinating Walt Disney by Stephen Schochet

The American Colonists Library; Treasury of Primary Source Documents Pertaining to Early American History.

Website: www.1771.org/cd_recipes.htm (The Claude Moore Colonial Farm at Turkey Run)

Google.com

Www.bartleby.com

Www.usmemorialday.org

Weekly Reader Magazine

Answer to Geography Logic Puzzle:

Clue 1 There are clues in the directions.

Lucy and I left Detroit together, that means we started out in Michigan. We were never in the same state again until we met at our final destination, so if Lucy visited a state, then I must not have visited it, and if I visited a state, then Lucy must not have.

Clue 2 I started out going northwest, all the way to the Pacific Ocean in fact. My first stop was in a state that starts with the same letter as the state that Lucy first visited. Then, I headed south just one state and almost caught up with Lucy, but ended up in the state right next to the one she was in on her second stop, which was only one state west of where she was on her first stop.

Northwest from Michigan to the Pacific must be Washington (all other states on the Pacific would be straight west or southwest of Michigan). Lucy went to a state with the same letter (W). The choices are Wisconsin, West Virginia, and Wyoming. She can't go to Washington because I did (Clue #1). If I go south one state then I am in Oregon, and right next to Idaho (where Lucy made her second stop) which is only one state west of her first stop that starts with a W, and must by Wyoming.

Clue 3 Neither Lucy or I has ever left the contiguous United States. I flew east to Richmond, while Lucy went south to Phoenix.

This eliminates Alaska and Hawaii. Richmond is in Virginia and Phoenix is in Arizona.

Clue 4 I flew to the biggest state and Lucy went to the smallest state. We both wanted to see the Hersey factory, but neither of us ever made it to that state.

I went to Texas and Lucy went to Rhode Island. Hersey is in Pennsylvania.

Clue 5 Of the states that were left, I visited all the ones that start with the letter 'I' and ended up in the 'I' state farthest to the east, but neither I nor Lucy ever visited the four letter state right next to it.

The states that begin with I are Iowa, Illinois, Indiana and Idaho (eliminated in Clue #2). The farthest to the east is Indiana, and the neighboring state with four letters is Ohio.

Clue 6 Lucy has been to every state that begins with the letter 'm' and ended up in the 'm' state that is farthest to the south. Neither of us traveled to the state directly north or the one directly east of this 'm' state.

The M states are Massachusetts, Maryland, Maine Michigan (Clue #1), Minnesota, Missouri, Mississippi, and Montana. The one farthest to the south is Mississippi; directly north of that is Tennessee and east is Alabama.

Clue 7 Lucy and I each only visited one state each that touches the Gulf of Mexico, but I did visit a state with the same name as our country neighbor to the south.

We each visited one state on the Gulf, I went to Texas (Clue #4) and Lucy went to Mississippi (Clue #6), so neither of us went to Alabama (Clue #6), Louisiana, or Florida. Our country neighbor to the south is Mexico, so I went to New Mexico (state with the same name).

Clue 8 Neither of us ever visited a state with the word north, south, east or west in the name, but Lucy made her next stop in a large eastern state with the word NEW in it. Two other states with the word New were never visited at all.

This eliminates North Dakota, South Dakota, North Carolina, South Carolina, and West Virginia. A large eastern state with the word New is New York. There are three other states with the word New in them; New Mexico (visited by me Clue #7), New Hampshire, and New Jersey. The two that were never visited are New Hampshire and New Jersey.

Clue 9 Our final destination was not Colorado or any state that touches it.

Eliminate Colorado. The states that touch it are Utah, Oklahoma, Kansas, Nebraska, Arizona (Clue #3), New Mexico (Clue #7) and Wyoming (Clue #2).

Clue 10 Lucy's longest flight went from Vermont to California. Her shortest flight went from Wisconsin to Arkansas. Neither of these was her final flight.

Lucy went to Vermont, California, Wisconsin and Arkansas. None of these was the final destination.

Clue 11 My longest flight went from Connecticut to Nevada. My shortest flight went from Georgia to Kentucky. Neither of these was my last flight.

I went to Connecticut, Nevada, Georgia, and Kentucky. None of these was the final destination. The only state left is Delaware.

Acknowledgments

Let me begin by saying the Walt Disney World, Magic Kingdom, and all the other words and phrases associated to that, such as, but not limited to the names of the lands, names of the attractions, phrases like Imagineers, streetmosphere, and cast members are trademarked, registered, copyrighted and so on... the sole property of Disney Co. We don't work for them, we didn't ask for permission to talk about them, study their parks or even use their name in this conversation, they didn't pay us to write this, we didn't pay them to let us, and so on, etcetera, etcetera, ad infinitum. That said...

We would not be able to even think about putting out this second book in the Vacation Education series if it wasn't for the financial support of all the families who have purchased Vacation Education destination Epcot. Thank You!

Of course, it also needs to be said that there would be no Vacation Education Books at all if it hadn't been planned by God Almighty to be that way.

Additional thanks to my husband Don, who had so much faith in this project that he quit his job to come home and give me time to finish this second book. Thanks to my friend Sue Battel and the staff at Color House Graphics, especially Linda Doxtater, who encouraged me every step of the way, and patiently answered my unending list of questions.

Also, thanks to my mom who in the beginning bought more copies than any bookstore, and bragged about me to all her friends, and even gave us money to keep things going when we weren't sure we would make it otherwise.

Particularly, I thank God for providing friends and family who supported us in so many ways, who fed us and clothed us, who listened to our stories, who helped us prepare our presentations, and for odd jobs that kept the trickle coming in to pay the bills as we worked to build this ministry.

And, last, but certainly not least, I am thankful for you, dear reader, who has chosen to purchase this book, and who hopefully has made a decision to make the most of your time with your family. Happy Travels to you!

Please Write to Us at
Vacation Education Books
318 W. Upton Ave.
Reed City, MI 49677

Or visit us online at vacationeducationbooks.com